The Language Revolution

THEMES FOR THE 21ST CENTURY

Titles in this series

The Language Revolution

DAVID CRYSTAL

polity

First published in 2004 by Polity Press Ltd.

Polity Press
65 Bridge Street
Cambridge CB2 1UR, UK

Polity Press
350 Main Street
Malden, MA 02148, USA

ISBN: 0-7456-3312-9
ISBN: 0-7456-3313-7 (pb)

A catalogue record for this book is available from the British
Library and has been applied for from the Library of Congress.

Typeset in 10.5 on 12 pt Plantin
by Kolam Information Services Pvt. Ltd
Printed and bound in Great Britain by TJ International,
Padstow, Cornwall

For further information on Polity, visit our website:
www.polity.co.uk

Contents

Preface

The Language Revolution is an attempt to see further by
standing on the shoulders of three of my books published
between 1997 and 2001: *English as a Global Language,
Language Death* and *Language and the Internet.* The topics
evolved as a trilogy, but it was only after the third book was
completed that the complementarity of their themes
became apparent to me. The present book highlights the
interrelationship between them, and takes a view about the
contemporary significance of the language trends they
discuss.

I have been faced with a literary problem, as a consequence, and I hope my solution is acceptable. Because the
'Themes for the 21st Century' series is aimed at a general
readership, I have assumed that readers will *not* be familiar
with the earlier books. The first three chapters, accordingly, incorporate summaries of the three arguments. This
will generate a strong sense of déjà vu among those readers
– I imagine, mainly linguists and language professionals –
who *have* read them, for which I apologize. But the present
account was not written with them primarily in mind.

The 'Themes for the 21st Century' series also likes to
keep references and notes to a minimum, and so my few
notes are here chiefly to provide a source for the occasional
quotation. The downside of this procedure is that, if

readers want to investigate the basis of my observations in further detail, they will have to go to the earlier books, which contain several hundred footnotes and bibliographical references – though in the case of *English as a Global Language*, these appear only in the second edition, published in 2003.

David Crystal
Holyhead, September 2003

Acknowledgements

The following poems by R.S. Thomas, reprinted in his *Collected Poems 1954–90* (London: Phoenix Press, 2001), are reproduced by kind permission of Gwydion Thomas (© Kunjana Thomas 2001): 'Drowning', originally published in *Welsh Airs* (Bridgend: Poetry Wales Press, 1987); 'It Hurts Him to Think', originally published in *What is a Welshman?* (Swansea: Christopher Davies, 1974); and 'Reservoirs', originally published in *Not That He Brought Flowers* (London: Rupert Hart-Davies, 1968).

Introduction: A New Linguistic World

The year 2000 marked the end of a decade of linguistic revolution. The new century must deal with its consequences.

Few people noticed at the time. But then, language change is like that – taking place slowly and subtly, unpredictable in its outcome, and recognized only after some time has passed. Most of us take language very much for granted, in any case, and are not used to bringing it into the forefront of our attention. And as revolutions affecting language do not happen very often in human history, it isn't obvious what to look out for when one does come along. Even the language professionals – the practitioners of linguistics – took until the end of the decade to draw public attention to the unprecedented nature of the various events they were observing. And we still lack integrated accounts of what happened – this book is a first attempt. But once we stand back and reflect on the dramatic linguistic changes which took place during the 1990s, the case that we are living at the beginning of a new linguistic era is, I believe, unassailable.

You might have guessed that Something Was Up if you had noticed that 2001 was designated the European Year of Languages. This was the first time a whole year had been devoted to languages, and although it was being celebrated only in Europe, it was ambitiously general in its aims. It was not, after all, called the Year of European Languages – in the sense of 'languages indigenous to Europe'. *All* languages spoken in Europe were included in its remit – and that meant dozens of African and Asian languages used by minorities all over the Continent. It was a year which focused on the importance of language as an expression of cultural identity, as a medium of inter-national and national intelligibility, and as a means of enabling individuals and countries to open doors to a wider cultural and commercial world. It might just as easily have been called the European Year of Language. The acronym would have been the same: EYL.

Many events took place in many countries during that year, and one of the outcomes was the establishment of 26 September as an annual World Language Day, to keep public attention focused on the importance of plurilingual-ism – or, if you prefer, multilingualism – and foreign lan-guage learning. It was the second such decision. In 1999, UNESCO had already created 21 February as International Mother Language Day – a date which commemorated the deaths on that date in 1952 of five students defending the recognition of Bangla as a state language of former Pakistan (now Bangladesh). Here too the aim was to protect and promote linguistic diversity and multilingual education. Two 'days' devoted to language within three years! Lan-guages had never received such limelight before. Was it a coincidence that the momentum for such outcomes gathered pace so successfully during the mid-nineties? If a language revolution was taking place, then probably not. This is precisely the kind of practical outcome we would expect to see if people were deriving fresh motivation and enthusiasm from a growing sense of new linguistic energies.

I do not believe that 'revolution' is too strong a word for what has been taking place. A 'revolution' is any combin-

ation of events which produces a radical shift in consciousness or behaviour over a relatively short period of time,
and this is what has happened. There are always continu-
ities with the past, but these are outweighed by the emergence of a genuinely fresh perspective. In the context of an
individual language, revolutions are rare. In the history of
English, for example, we might identify two, only, since
the arrival of the language in Britain in the fifth century.
First, in the early Middle Ages, there was the combination
of linguistic developments and sociopolitical factors which
around the eleventh century changed Old English to
Middle English, with very different grammar, and an ad-
mixture of Romance elements that profoundly affected
spelling and vocabulary – a revolution which took us, in
effect, from *Beowulf* to Chaucer. Then there was the period
in the fifteenth century which took us from Chaucer to
Shakespeare, resulting in an Early Modern English which
was very different from its Middle English predecessor in
grammar, sounds and spelling, and characterized especially by the standardizing effect of printing and the cumu-
lative impact of the Renaissance, with its vast influx of
classical vocabulary. Since Shakespeare, the language has
developed steadily, but its character has not been radically
altered – as is evidenced by the fact that we can go to a
Shakespeare play and understand most of what we encounter. It is patently 'the same' language – an intuition
we do not have so comfortably when we encounter Chaucer,
and not at all when we try to read *Beowulf*.

Many other languages have displayed their own periods
of revolutionary change, but these have occurred at different times and for different reasons. The wars, alliances and
political revolutions that cause massive social (and thus
linguistic) change do not follow any shared or predictable
timetable. The French Revolution had major consequences for both French and the minority languages of

France, but little linguistic impact elsewhere. The Russian Revolution, likewise, led to policies which seriously affected the maintenance of regional and minority languages in the Soviet Union; but again, with negligible impact outside. It is unusual to find changes which are so broad in their implications that they affect groups of languages, and extremely rare to find changes which are so global that they affect all languages. Indeed, to illustrate the last point we have to alter the level of the illustration and refer to the arrival of new media – such as writing, printing, telephony and broadcasting – whose influence on the character of languages has been universal. The Internet is the latest of these media, and its impact on language – as we shall see in chapter 3 – has been the most revolutionary of all. This is a case where there is so little continuity with previous communicative behaviour that the term 'revolution' is especially well motivated – and, indeed, is in danger of being overused.

What makes the second half of the twentieth century – and the 1990s in particular – a highly significant period in the history of language is that we can find there a coming together of three major trends, each global in its implications, which together have fundamentally altered the world's linguistic ecology. It is the combined impact of these trends, affecting all languages in unprecedented ways, which warrants my use of the epithet 'revolutionary'. I have written separately on each of them, but this is the first attempt to bring them together into a single frame of reference, and to explore the consequences for the future of languages in particular and of language in general. In *English as a Global Language* (1997), I discussed the reasons for the emergence of English as the world's first truly global language, and the dramatic effect this new-found status is having on English itself. The future of English is not as clear-cut as might be assumed – an argument I review in chapter 1. *Language Death* (2000) presented the crisis facing huge numbers of languages which are currently endangered or dying, and reported the fresh initiatives being taken towards preservation and regeneration. Here we are faced with the probable loss this century of at least half the world's languages, raising issues which are taken up in chapter 2. And in *Language and the Internet* (2001), I examined the radical effect on language of the arrival of Internet technology, which has supplemented spoken and written language with a linguistically novel medium of communication, and raised fresh questions about the way language will continue to evolve. These issues are reviewed in chapter 3.

The three topics are usually discussed separately, as these books illustrate, with points of interconnection referred to only in passing. When we examine them together, and focus on the interrelationships, we encounter a vision of a linguistic future which is radically different from what has existed in the past. It is a future where we will need to revise many cherished concepts relating to the way we think about and work with languages. Some pointers towards the nature of the revision are brought together in chapters 4 and 5. The concerns turn out to be general, going well beyond the responsibilities of linguists, language teachers and others professionally engaged in the language 'business', and involving sectors of society not traditionally considered to have much connection with linguistic affairs. But that is the nature of revolutions. They affect everyone.

1

The Future of Englishes

The emergence of English as a genuine world language is the earliest of the three trends which achieved especial prominence during the 1990s. The word 'genuine' is crucial. The possibility that English might evolve a global role had been recognized as early as the eighteenth century. In 1780 the future US president John Adams said: 'English is destined to be in the next and succeeding centuries more generally the language of the world than Latin was in the last or French is in the present age.'[1] But it took nearly 200 years before he was proved right. Only a relatively short time ago the prospect of English becoming a truly global language was uncertain. Indeed, it was only in the 1990s that the issue really came to the fore, with surveys, books and conferences trying to explain how it is that a language can become truly global, what the consequences are when it happens, and why English has become the prime candidate.[2] But, in order to speculate about the future of English – or, as I shall explain below, Englishes – we must first understand where we are now, and how the present situation has arisen.

The present

A characterization, to begin with; then some statistics. A language does not achieve a genuinely global status until it develops a special role that is recognized in every country. This role will be most obvious in countries where large numbers of the people speak it as a first language – in the case of English, this would mean the USA, Canada, Britain, Ireland, Australia, New Zealand, South Africa, several Caribbean countries and a scattering of other territories. However, no language has ever been spoken by a mother-tongue majority in more than a dozen or so countries, so mother-tongue use by itself cannot give a language global status. To achieve such a status, a language has to be taken up by other countries around the world. They must decide to give it a special place within their communities, even though they may have few (or no) mother-tongue speakers.

There are two main ways in which this can be done. First, the language can be made the official (or semi-official) language of a country, to be used as a medium of communication in such domains as government, the law courts, the media and the educational system. To get on in such societies, it is essential to master the official language as early in life as possible. This role is well illustrated by English, which as a result of British or American history now has some kind of special administrative status in over seventy countries, such as Ghana, Nigeria, India, Singapore and Vanuatu. This is far more than the status achieved by any other language (French being closest). Second, the language can be made a priority in a country's foreign-language teaching. It becomes the language which children are most likely to be taught when they arrive in school, and the one most available to adults who – for whatever reason – never learned it, or learned it badly, in their early educational years. Over 100 countries treat English as just such a foreign language; and in most of these it is now recognized as the chief foreign language to be taught in schools.

Because of this three-pronged development – of first-language, second-language and foreign-language speakers – it is inevitable that a world language will eventually come to be used by more people than any other language. English has now reached this stage. Those who have learned it as a first language are estimated to be around 400 million – though estimates vary greatly, because few countries keep statistics about numbers of speakers. Those who have learned it as a second language are also difficult to estimate, for now we must take into account the levels of fluency achieved. If we take a basic level of conversational ability as the criterion – enough to make yourself understood, though by no means free of errors, and with little command of specialized vocabulary – the figure is also some 400 million. The significance of these two figures should not be missed: as many people now use English as a second language as use it as a mother-tongue. And because the population growth in areas where English is a second language is about three times that in areas where it is a first language, second-language speakers of English will soon hugely exceed first-language speakers – a situation without precedent for an international language. When the number of people who speak English as a foreign language is taken into account, this contrast becomes even more dramatic. Here too estimates are uncertain – no-one knows, for example, how many people are learning English in China – but the British Council has estimated that roughly a billion people are learning English around the world at any one time. Excluding the complete beginners, it would seem reasonable to take two-thirds of these as a guess at the number of foreign learners with whom it would be possible to hold a reasonable conversation in English – say 600 million.

If, now, we add the three totals – the 400 million or so who use it as a first language, plus the 400 million or so who use it as a second language, and the 600 million or so who use it as a foreign language – we will end up with a grand total of about 1,400 million. This in round terms is a quarter of the world's population (just over 6,000 million in 2000). No other language is used so extensively – either numerically, or with such geographical reach. Even Chinese, found in eight different spoken languages, but unified by a common writing system, is known to 'only' some 1,100 million, and most of these are mother-tongue speakers in a few territories. Of course, we must not overstate the situation. If one in four of the world's population speaks English, three out of four do not. We do not have to travel far into the hinterland of a country – away from the tourist spots, the airports, the hotels, the restaurants – to encounter this reality. But even so, one in four is impressive, and unprecedented. And we must ask: Why? It is not so much the total, as the speed with which this expansion has taken place, very largely since the 1950s. What can account for it?

An obvious factor, of course, is the need for a common language, or *lingua franca* – a concept probably as old as language itself. But the prospect that a lingua franca might be needed for the whole world is something which has emerged strongly only in the twentieth century, and since the 1950s in particular. The chief international forum for political communication – the United Nations – dates only from 1945, and then it had only fifty-one member states. By 1960 this had risen to over eighty members. But the independence movements which began at that time led to a massive increase in the number of new nations during the next decade, and this process continued steadily into the 1990s. In 2003 there were 191 members in the UN – nearly four times as many as there were fifty years ago. The need for lingua francas is obvious, and pressure to find a single lingua franca is a consequence, the alternative being expensive and often impracticable multi-way translation facilities.

The past

But why English? There is of course nothing intrinsically wonderful about the English language that it should have spread in this way. Its pronunciation is not simpler than that of many other languages, its grammar is no simpler – what it lacks in morphology (in cases and genders) it certainly makes up for in syntax (in word-order patterns) – and its spelling certainly isn't simpler. A language becomes a world language for one reason only – the power of the people who speak it. But power means different things: it can mean political (military) power, technological power, economic power and cultural power. Each of these influenced the growth of English at different times. Political power emerged in the form of the colonialism that brought English around the world from the sixteenth century, so that by the nineteenth century, the language was one 'on which the sun never sets'. Technological power is associated with the Industrial Revolution of the eighteenth and nineteenth centuries, when over half of the scientists and technologists who made that revolution worked through the medium of English, and people who travelled to Britain (and later America) to learn about the new technologies inevitably had to do so through English. The nineteenth century saw the growth in the economic power of the United States, rapidly over-taking Britain as its population hugely grew, and adding greatly to the number of world English speakers. The point was recognized by Bismarck as early as 1898: asked by a journalist what he considered to be the decisive factor in modern history, he is said to have replied, 'The fact that the North Americans speak English.'[3] And in the twenti-eth century, we indeed saw the fourth kind of power, cultural power, manifesting itself in virtually every walk of life through spheres of chiefly American influence.

As a result of these different manifestations of power, it is possible to recognize ten domains in which English has become pre-eminent.

Politics

Most pre-twentieth-century commentators would have had no difficulty giving a single, political answer to the question, 'Why world English?' They would simply have pointed to the growth of the British Empire. This legacy carried over into the last century. The League of Nations was the first of many modern international alliances to allocate a special place to English in its proceedings: Eng-lish was one of the two official languages (the other was French), and all documents were printed in both. I have already mentioned the UN, which replaced it. But English now plays an official or working role in the proceedings of most other major international political gatherings, in all parts of the world. The extent to which English is used in this way is often not appreciated. According to recent issues of the *Union of International Associations' Yearbook*, there are about 12,500 international organizations in the world. A sample showed that 85 per cent made official use of English – far more than any other language. French was the only other to show up strongly, with 49 per cent using it officially.

International politics operates at several levels and in many different ways, but the presence of English is usually not far away. A political protest may surface in the form of an official question to a government minister, a peaceful lobby outside an embassy, a street riot or a bomb. When the television cameras present the event to a world audience, it is notable how often a message in English can be seen on a banner or placard as part of the occasion. Whatever the mother-tongue of the protesters, they know that their cause will gain maximum impact if it is expressed through the medium of English. A famous instance of this occurred a few years ago in India, where a march supporting Hindi and opposing English was seen on world television: most of the banners were in Hindi, but one astute marcher carried a prominent sign which enabled the voice of his group to reach much further around the world than would otherwise have been possible. His sign read: 'Death to English.'

Economics

By the beginning of the nineteenth century, Britain had become the world's leading industrial and trading nation. Its population of 5 million in 1700 more than doubled by 1800, and during that century no country could equal its economic growth, with a gross national product rising, on average, at 2 per cent per year. By 1800, the chief growth areas, in textiles and mining, were producing a range of manufactured goods for export which led to Britain becoming known as the 'workshop of the world'. Steam technology revolutionized printing, generating an unprecedented mass of publications in English. The early nineteenth century saw the rapid growth of the international banking system, especially in Germany, Britain and the USA, with London and New York becoming the world's investment capitals. In 1914, Britain and the USA were together investing over $10 billion abroad – three times as much as France and almost four times as much as Germany. The resulting 'economic imperialism' brought a fresh dimension to the balance of linguistic power. 'Money talks' was the chief metaphor – and the language in which it was talking was chiefly English.

The press

The English language has been an important medium of the press for nearly 400 years. The nineteenth century was the period of greatest progress, thanks to the introduction of new printing technology and new methods of mass production and transportation. It also saw the development of a truly independent press, chiefly fostered in the USA, where there were some 400 daily newspapers by 1850, and nearly 2,000 by the turn of the century. Censorship and other restrictions continued in Continental Europe during the early decades, however, which meant that the provision of popular news in languages other than English developed much more slowly. Today, about a third of the world's newspapers are published in countries where English has special status, and the majority of these will be in English.

The high profile given to English in the popular press was reinforced by the way techniques of news gathering developed. The mid-nineteenth century saw the growth of the major news agencies, especially following the invention of the telegraph. Paul Julius Reuter started an office in Aachen, but soon moved to London, where in 1851 he launched the agency which now bears his name. By 1870 Reuters had acquired more territorial news monopolies than any of its Continental competitors. With the emergence in 1856 of the New York Associated Press, the majority of the information being transmitted along the telegraph wires of the world was in English.

Advertising

Towards the end of the nineteenth century, a combination of social and economic factors led to a dramatic increase in the use of advertisements in publications, especially in the more industrialized countries. Mass production had increased the flow of goods and was fostering competition; consumer purchasing power was growing; and new printing techniques were providing fresh display possibilities. In the USA, publishers realized that income from advertising would allow them to lower the selling price of their magazines, and thus hugely increase circulation. Two-thirds of a modern newspaper, especially in the USA, may be devoted to advertising. During the nineteenth century the advertising slogan became a feature of the medium, as did the famous 'trade name'. 'It pays to advertise' itself became a US slogan in the 1920s. Many products which are now household names received a special boost in that decade, such as those produced by Ford, Coca Cola, Kodak and Kellogg. The media capitalized on the brevity with which a product could be conveyed to an audience – even if the people were passing at speed in one of the new methods of transportation. Posters, billboards, electric displays, shop signs and other techniques became part of the everyday scene. As international markets grew, the 'outdoor media' began to travel the world, and their prominence in virtually every town and city is now one of the most noticeable global manifestations of English language use. The English advertisements are not always more numerous in countries where

English has no special status, but they are usually the most apparent. American English ruled: by 1972, only three of the world's top thirty advertising agencies were not US-owned.

Broadcasting

It took many decades of experimental research in physics, chiefly in Britain and America, before it was possible to send the first radio telecommunication signals through the air, without wires. Marconi's system, built in 1895, carried telegraph code signals over a distance of one mile. Six years later, his signals had crossed the Atlantic Ocean; by 1918, they had reached Australia. English was the first language to be transmitted by radio. Within twenty-five years of Marconi's first transmission, public broadcasting became a reality. The first commercial radio station, in Pittsburgh, Pennsylvania, broadcast its first programme in November 1920, and there were over 500 broadcasting stations licensed in the USA within two years. A similar dramatic expansion affected public television twenty years later. We can only speculate about how these media developments must have influenced the growth of world English. There are no statistics on the proportion of time devoted to English-language programmes the world over, or on how much time is spent listening to such programmes. But if we look at broadcasting aimed specifically at audiences in other countries (such as the BBC World Service, or the Voice of America), we note significant levels of provision – over a thousand hours a week by the former, twice as much by the latter. Most other countries showed sharp increases in external broadcasting during the post-war years, and several launched English-language radio programmes, such as the Soviet Union, Italy, Japan, Luxembourg, the Netherlands, Sweden and Germany. No comparative data are available about how many people listen to each of the languages provided by these services. However, if we list the languages in which these countries broadcast, it is noticeable that only one of these languages has a place on each of the lists: English.

Motion pictures

The new technologies which followed the discovery of electrical power fundamentally altered the nature of home and public entertainment, and provided fresh directions for the development of the English language. The technology of this industry has many roots in Europe and America during the nineteenth century, with England and France providing an initial impetus to the artistic and commercial development of the cinema from 1895. However, the years preceding and during the First World War stunted the growth of a European film industry, and dominance soon passed to America, which oversaw from 1915 the emergence of the feature film, the star system, the movie mogul and the grand studio, all based in Hollywood. As a result, when sound was added to the technology in the late 1920s, it was the English language which suddenly came to dominate the movie world. And despite the growth of the film industry in other countries in later decades, English-language movies still dominate the medium, with Hollywood coming to rely increasingly on a small number of annual productions aimed at huge audiences. It is unusual to find a blockbuster movie produced in a language other than English, and about 80 per cent of all feature films given a theatrical release are in English. The influence of movies on the viewing audience is uncertain, but many observers agree with the view of director Wim Wenders: 'People increasingly believe in what they see and they buy what they believe in. . . . People use, drive, wear, eat and buy what they see in the movies.'[4] If this is so, then the fact that most movies are made in the English language must surely be significant, at least in the long term.

Popular music

The cinema was one of two new entertainment technologies which emerged at the end of the nineteenth century; the other was the recording industry. Here too the English language was early in evidence. When in 1877 Thomas A. Edison devised the phonograph, the first machine that could both record and reproduce sound, the first words to be recorded were 'What God hath wrought', followed by a recitation of the nursery-rhyme 'Mary had a little lamb'. Most of the subsequent technical developments took place in the USA. All the major recording companies in popular music had English-language origins, beginning with the US firm Columbia (from 1898). Radio sets around the world hourly testify to the dominance of English in the popular music scene today. Many people make their first contact with English in this way. By the turn of the century, Tin Pan Alley (the popular name for the Broadway-centred song-publishing industry) was a reality, and was soon known worldwide as the chief source of US popular music. Jazz, too, had its linguistic dimension, with the development of the blues and many other genres. And by the time modern popular music arrived, it was almost entirely an English scene. The pop stars of two chief English-speaking nations were soon to dominate the recording world: Bill Haley and the Comets and Elvis Presley in the USA; the Beatles and the Rolling Stones in the UK. Mass audiences for pop singers became a routine feature of the world scene from the 1960s. No other single source has spread the English language around the youth of the world so rapidly and so pervasively.

International travel and safety

The reasons for travelling abroad are many and various. Each journey has immediate linguistic consequences – a language has to be interpreted, learned, imposed – and over time a travelling trend can develop into a major influence. If there is a contemporary movement towards world English use, therefore, we would expect it to be particularly noticeable in this domain; and so it is. For those whose international travel brings them into a world of package holidays, business meetings, academic conferences, international conventions, community rallies, sporting occasions, military occupations and other 'official' gatherings, the domains of transportation and accommodation are chiefly mediated through the use of English as an auxiliary language. Safety instructions on international flights and sailings, information about emergency procedures in hotels, and directions to major locations are now routinely in English alongside local languages. Most notices which tell us to fasten our seatbelts, find the lifeboat stations or check the location of the emergency stairs give us an option in English.

A special aspect of safety is the way that the language has come to be used as a means of controlling international transport operations, especially on water and in the air. English has emerged as the international language of the sea, in the form of Essential English for International Maritime Use – often referred to as 'Seaspeak'. Progress has also been made in recent years in devising systems of unambiguous communication between organizations which are involved in handling emergencies on the ground – notably, the fire service, the ambulance service and the police. There is now 'Emergencyspeak', trying to cope with problems of ambiguity at the two ends of the Channel Tunnel. And of course there is 'Airspeak', the language of international aircraft control. This did not emerge until after the Second World War, when the International Civil Aviation Organization was created. Only then was it agreed that English should be the international language of aviation when pilots and controllers speak different languages. Over 180 nations have since adopted its recommendations about English terminology – though it should be noted that there is nothing mandatory about them.

Education

English is the medium of a great deal of the world's knowledge, especially in such areas as science and technology. And access to knowledge is the business of education. When we investigate why so many nations have in recent years made English an official language or chosen it as their chief foreign language in schools, one of the most important reasons is always educational – in the broadest sense. Sridath Ramphal, writing in 1996, provides a relevant illustration:

> Shortly after I became Secretary-General of the Commonwealth in 1975, I met Prime Minister Sirimavo Bandaranaike in Colombo and we talked of ways in which the Commonwealth Secretariat could help Sri Lanka. Her response was immediate and specific: 'Send us people to train our teachers to teach English as a foreign language.' My amazement must have showed, for the Prime Minister went on to explain that the policies her husband had put in place twenty years earlier to promote Sinhalese as the official language had succeeded so well that in the process Sri Lanka – so long the pearl of the English-speaking world in Asia – had in fact lost English, even as a second language

save for the most educated Sri Lankans. Her concern was
for development. Farmers in the field, she told me, could
not read the instructions on bags of imported fertiliser –
and manufacturers in the global market were not likely to
print them in Sinhalese. Sri Lanka was losing its access to
the world language of English.[5]

Since the 1960s, English has become the normal medium
of instruction in higher education for many countries –
including several where the language has no official status.
No African country uses its indigenous language in higher
education, English being used in the majority of cases. The
English language teaching (ELT) business has become
one of the major growth industries around the world in
the past thirty years.

Communications

If a language is a truly international medium, it is going to
be most apparent in those services which deal directly with
the task of communication – the postal and telephone
systems and the electronic networks. Information about
the use of English in these domains is not easy to come by,
however. It is thought that three-quarters of the world's
mail is in English. But as no-one monitors the language in
which we write our letters, such statistics are highly specu-
lative. Only on the Internet, where messages and data can
be left for indefinite periods of time, is it possible to
develop an idea of how much of the world's everyday
communications (at least, between computer-owners) is
actually in English. This domain will receive separate discussion in chapter 3, but the relevant point can be antici-
pated here. The Internet began life as an English-language
medium, and English has retained its dominance. It
started out as ARPANET, the Advanced Research Pro-

jects Agency network, in the late 1960s, conceived as a decentralized national network, its aim being to link important American academic and government institutions in a way which would survive local damage in the event of a major war. Its language was, accordingly, English; and when people in other countries began to form links with this network, it proved essential for them to use English. The dominance of this language was then reinforced when the service was opened up in the 1980s to private and commercial organizations, most of which were (for the reasons already given) already communicating chiefly in English. There was also a technical reason underpinning the position of the language at this time. The first protocols devised to carry data on the Net were developed for the English alphabet, and even today no browser is able to handle all aspects of multilingual data presentation. However, the number of non-English-language users on the Internet is growing all the time, and now exceeds the number of new English-speaking users. The consequences of this for minority languages are explored in chapter 3.

The future

When a language becomes a world language, what happens to it, and what happens to other languages as a consequence? There are no precedents, because no language has ever been spoken by so many people in so many countries before. But several major trends can already be seen, and each of them is going to play a significant role in forming the new linguistic climate of the twenty-first century.

However, before considering the case of English in greater detail, we should ask: is English going to continue in its present position, or is its global status likely to be challenged by other languages? History teaches us one thing: there are never grounds for complacency in considering a language's position. A thousand years ago, the position of Latin would have seemed unassailable. Who knows what the position of any language will be in a thousand years' time? Language status, as we have seen, is intimately bound up with political, military, economic and cultural power, and as these variables alter, so languages rise and fall. Futurologists do not find it difficult to envisage scenarios in which, for example, Arabic, Chinese or Spanish becomes the next world language. Spanish is in fact the world's fastest-growing mother-tongue at present. But for the foreseeable future, it is unlikely that another language is going to replace English in its global role. The factors which brought English to its present position are still very largely in place. English has achieved a presence and momentum which will be extremely difficult to dislodge. People continue to learn English in increasing numbers all over the world. Whatever the attitude towards the cultures who use it, the value of the language as a functional tool is widely accepted. Even those who are most opposed to it find themselves having to use it, if only to achieve a universal audience for their opposition. There is no real sign of this position weakening within the first decade of the new millennium.

English may be relatively stable in its world status, but it is certainly not stable in its linguistic character. Indeed, the language is currently changing more rapidly than at any time since the Renaissance. Several factors are involved, but the chief one is undoubtedly the change in the language's centre of gravity. It is a point often forgotten, especially by native speakers, that a language which has come to be spoken by so many people has ceased to be owned by any of its constituent communities – not the

British, with whom the language began 1,500 years ago, nor the Americans, who now comprise its largest mother-tongue community. The total number of mother-tongue speakers in the world, some 400 million, as seen above, is actually falling, as a proportion of world English users, because of the differential in population growth between first-language countries and those where English is a second or foreign language. Three out of four English speakers are now non-native.

All these users have a share in the future of English. Language is an immensely democratizing institution. To have learned a language is immediately to have rights in it. You may add to it, modify it, play with it, create in it, ignore bits of it, as you will. And it is just as likely that the future course of English is going to be influenced by those who speak it as a second or foreign language as by those who speak it as a mother-tongue. Fashions count, in language, as anywhere else; and fashions are a function of numbers. It is perfectly possible for a linguistic fashion to be started by a group of second-language or foreign-language learners, or by those who speak a nonstandard variety, which then catches on among mother-tongue speakers. Rapping is a recent case in point. And as numbers grow, and second/foreign-language speakers gain in national and international prestige, usages which were previously criticized as 'foreign' – such as *three person, he be running, many informations* – can become part of the standard educated speech of a locality, and eventually appear in writing. An example is *Welcome in Egypt*, which has come to be widely used in that country, and now appears in English textbooks there. The biggest thing that native speakers of English are going to have to get used to, in the twenty-first century, is that they are no longer in charge of language trends. The English language as spoken in Britain is now a minority dialect of World

English – amounting to some 4 per cent of the global English-speaking population. Even speakers of English in the USA only amount to some 15 per cent of the world total. In India, there are probably now more speakers of English than in the whole of Britain and the USA combined.

What happens when large numbers of people adopt English in a country? They develop an English of their own. There are now many new varieties of spoken English developing around the world, in such countries as India, Singapore and Ghana. They have been called 'New Englishes'. Why have they arisen? Because of the need to express national identity. Imagine the situation in one of the newly independent nations of the 1950s and 1960s. With newfound independence comes an urge to manifest identity in the eyes of the world. And one of the most important ways of manifesting this identity is through the medium of the language. So, which language will you use? Many of the new countries, such as Ghana and Nigeria, found that they had no alternative but to continue using English – the alternative was to make an impossible choice between the many competing local ethnic languages – over 400, in the case of Nigeria. However, we can also appreciate the widely held feeling that to continue with English would be an unacceptable link with the colonial past. So how could this dilemma be resolved? The solution was for a country to continue with English, but to shape the language to meet its own ends – in particular, by adding local vocabulary, focusing on local cultural variations, and developing new forms of pronunciation. It is a largely unconscious process, of course, but promoted by local initiatives, such as regional dictionary surveys. It is not difficult to quickly accumulate several thousand local words, in countries which have a wide range of local fauna and flora, diverse ethnic customs and regular daily contacts with different languages. The emerging literatures of the Commonwealth countries – the novels from West Africa, India or South-east Asia, the poetry from the countries of the Caribbean – illustrate how quickly new identities can emerge. The term 'New Englishes' reflects these identities.

When a language spreads, it changes. The simple fact that parts of the world differ from each other so much physically and culturally means that speakers have innumerable opportunities to adapt the language to meet their communicative needs and to achieve fresh identities. The bulk of the adaptation will be in vocabulary – not just new words, but new meanings of words, and new idiomatic phrases – as this is the area which most closely reflects living conditions and ways of thinking. There is a country's bio-geographical uniqueness, which will generate potentially large numbers of words for animals, fish, birds, plants, rocks, and so on – and all the issues to do with land management and interpretation. There will be words for foodstuffs, drinks, medicines, drugs and the practices associated with eating, health-care, disease and death. The country's mythology and religion, and practices in astronomy and astrology, will bring forth new names for personalities, beliefs and rituals. Oral and perhaps also written literature will give rise to distinctive names in sagas, poems, oratory and folktales. There will be a body of local laws and customs, with their own terminology. The culture will have its own technology which will have its technical terms – such as for vehicles, house-building, weapons, clothing, ornaments and musical instruments. The world of leisure and the arts will have a linguistic dimension – names of dances, musical styles, games, sports – as will distinctiveness in body appearance – such as hair styles, tattoos, decoration. Virtually any aspect of social structure can generate complex naming systems – local government, family relationships, clubs and societies, and so on.

So, when a community adopts a new language, and starts to use it in relation to all areas of life, there is inevitably going to be a great deal of lexical adaptation. It only takes a year or so for the process to begin. The first permanent English settlement in North America was in Jamestown, Virginia, in 1607; and loan words from Native American languages were introduced into contemporary writing virtually immediately. Captain John Smith, writing in 1608, describes a *racoon*; *totem* is found in 1609; *caribou* and *opossum* are mentioned in 1610. Here is a recent example from an edition of the South African *Sunday Times* in the 1990s: 'Diplomatic indabas only rarely produce neatly wrapped solutions to problems.' *Indaba*, from Nguni, was originally a tribal conference, but has now been extended to mean any conference between political groups. These are examples of words being borrowed from local indigenous languages. In addition, some words will change their meaning, as they come to be applied to new settings and take on different senses. This has often happened in the language's history: for example, in the Anglo-Saxon period Christian missionaries took over pagan words (such as *heaven*, *hell*, *God* and *Easter*) and gave them new meanings. Today we see it in the way a biological species in the new country similar in appearance to one found in the old will often keep the old name, even though it is not the same entity – *pheasant* in South Africa is usually found for certain species of francolin. Every area of society is affected. *Robot* is the South African term for traffic-light.

How many words will grow in these ways? It does not take long before word-lists and dictionaries contain several thousand entries. There were over 3,000 items recorded in the first edition of *A Dictionary of South African English* (1978). *The Concise Australian National Dictionary* (1989) has 10,000 items in it. There are over 15,000 entries in the

Dictionary of Jamaican English (1967).[6] English speakers have always adopted an inclusive attitude towards loan words. English is a vacuum-cleaner of a language, readily sucking in words from whichever other languages it meets – well over 350 of them in the history of British English. Because of this, although English is historically a Germanic language, the bulk of its vocabulary is not – it is largely Classical and Romance in origin, with Greek, Latin and French loans especially important. And its diversified lexical character is especially increasing in parts of the world where there are many contact languages. In Nigeria, where over 400 source languages are available, the eventual lexical distinctiveness of Nigerian English is bound to be considerable.

The totals are small compared with the size of English vocabulary as a whole, which is well over a million words; but the effect of even fairly small numbers of localized words can be great. The new words are likely to be frequently used within the local community, precisely because they relate to distinctive notions there. Also, these words tend not to occur in isolation: if a conversation is about, say, local politics, then several political terms are likely to come together, making it impenetrable to outsiders. 'Blairite MP in New Labour Sleaze Trap, say Tories' might be a British newspaper example. Six words with British political meanings or overtones are found in quick succession, and the sentence will not be immediately interpretable to anyone unfamiliar with the world of British political discourse. Exactly the same kind of piling up of alien expressions can be found in areas where New Englishes are emerging. In this example from the South African *Sunday Times*, all the local words are Afrikaans in origin: 'It is interesting to recall that some verkrampte Nationalists, who pose now as super Afrikaners, were once bittereinder bloedsappe' [*verkramp*, bigoted; *bittereinder*, die-hard; *bloedsappe*, staunch member of the United Party, formerly the South African Party, or SAP].

It is easy to see how things might develop further. It wasn't just an Afrikaans noun which was distinctive in this last example; it was a noun phrase – a combination of adjective and noun. So, if a phrase, why not something bigger than a phrase? Add a verb on, perhaps, or make it a whole clause – in much the same way as in English we might borrow a whole sentence from French and say *Je ne sais quoi* or *c'est la vie*. Parts of an originally English sentence can easily come to contain large chunks of borrowed language. And in many parts of the world, where English is a second or foreign language, it is precisely this process which has been used with unprecedented frequency. People using English, even at a fairly advanced level, become stuck for a word, phrase or sentence; or, although using English as a lingua franca, find that a particular utterance in their mother-tongue suits better what they want to say. If they are talking to someone from their own language background, there is no problem in switching into the other language to solve the communication problem. A dialogue may move out of English, then back in again, several times in quick succession. The same situation obtains the other way round, too: people begin in their mother-tongue, then switch into English when they find their first language does not allow them to say what they want. This often happens when they get onto a subject-matter which they have learned only in English, such as computing – or even having a baby. I know a French-speaking mother who had a baby while living in Britain for a year. Back in France, she found herself switching into English every time she wanted to talk about the experience – much to the confusion of her French friends, whose baby-bearing experience had been resolutely francophone.

When people rely simultaneously on two or more languages to communicate with each other, the phenomenon is called *code-switching*. We can hear it happening now all over the world, between all sorts of languages, and it is on the increase. Because English is so widespread, it is especially noticeable there, in writing as well as in speech. In *The English Languages*, Tom McArthur gives an example of a bilingual leaflet issued by the HongkongBank in 1994 for Filipino workers. The Tagalog section contains a great deal of English mixed in. For example:

> Mg-deposito ng pera mula sa ibang HongkongBank account, at any Hongkongbank ATM, using your Cash Card. Mag-transfer ng regular amount bawa't buwan (by Standing Instruction) galang sa inyong Current o Savings Account, whether the account is with HongkongBank or not.[7]

This kind of language is often described using a compound name – in this case, Taglish (for Tagalog-English). We also have Franglais, Tex-Mex (for the Mexican Spanish used in Texas), Japlish, Spanglish, Chinglish, Denglish (Deutsch English), Wenglish (Welsh English), and many more. Traditionally, these names were used as scornful appellations. People would sneer at Tex-Mex, and say it was neither one language nor the other. It was 'gutter-speak', by people who had not learned to talk properly, or 'lazy-speak', by people who were letting themselves be too much influenced by English. But in the new century, we are going to have to rethink. We can hardly call a language like Taglish gutter-speak when it is being used in writing by a major banking corporation! Linguists have spent a lot of time analysing these 'mixed' languages, and found that they are full of complexity and subtlety of expression – as we would expect if people have the resources of two languages to draw upon.

Mixed languages are on the increase as we travel the English-speaking world; and it is important to realize the extent to which this is happening. They will probably be the main linguistic trend of the twenty-first century. Code-switching is already a normal feature of communication in the speech of millions who have learned English as a second or foreign language. I live in a Welsh-speaking part of Wales, and I hear code-switching between Welsh and English around me all the time. Indeed, globally, there are probably now more people who use English with some degree of code-switching than people who do not. And if these speakers are in the majority, or at least represented by significant numbers – as in the case of India – our traditional view of the language has to change. It is quite wrong to think of the 'future of World English' as if it is simply going to be a more widely used version of British English, or of American English. These varieties will stay, of course, but they will be supplemented by other varieties which, although perhaps originating in Britain or the USA, will display increasing differences from them.

The evidence of linguistic diversification – new Eng-lishes, with increased code-mixing – has been around a long time, but the extent of its presence has only recently come to be appreciated. It is not something we usually see in print – except insofar as a novelist captures it in a conversation, or it turns up in informal writing in a news-paper. But we readily encounter it when we travel to the countries concerned – usually in the form of a breakdown of comprehension. We speak to somebody in English, and they reply – but we cannot understand what they are saying, because their English is so different. And we ain't seen nothin' yet. All over the world, children are being born to parents with different first-language backgrounds who speak English as a lingua franca. Their English often contains a great deal of code-mixing or nonstandard usage.

If these parents choose to speak to their children in this English, as often happens, we now have the prospect of code-mixed and nonstandard English being learned as a mother-tongue – and by millions of the world's future citizens. The distinction between English as a first language and English as a foreign language ceases to be significant in such cases.

With these trends in mind, can we avoid the conclusion that, left to itself, English is going to fragment into mutually unintelligible varieties, just as Vulgar Latin did a millennium ago? The forces of the past fifty years, which have led to so many newly independent nation-states, certainly suggest this outcome. English has come to be used, in several of these countries, as the expression of a socio-political identity, and received a new character as a consequence, conventionally given such names as Nigerian English and Singaporean English. And if significant change can be noticed within a relatively short period of time – a few decades – must not these varieties become even more differentiated over the next century, so that we end up with an English 'family of languages'? An answer suggests itself if we examine the apparent parallel with Latin.

Latin revisited?

The parallels between the situations of English and Latin are certainly striking. During the first millennium, Latin became the universal language of educated European society – though we need to say Latins, for in Europe at that time it existed in several varieties. There was the prestige variety – the classical literary Latin written throughout the Roman Empire (chiefly in the West). Then there were the everyday spoken varieties of the language, referred to now as Vulgar Latin. Even as early as the first century BC, we find Cicero commenting on the provincial pronunciation heard in the Latin spoken in Cisalpine Gaul. By the eighth century, there is evidence of considerable shift, so much so that the way of referring to the language was changing: the 'lingua latina' was being described as 'lingua romana' or 'rustica romana lingua'. Certainly, by c.900, when we find the first texts representing the spoken language of Gaul, we can no longer talk of Latin, but must speak of Old French; and the other Romance languages begin to emerge at around the same time.

The situation facing Latin then was very similar to the situation facing English now. On the one hand, there was written Classical Latin, apparently alive and well and being taught in a standard way throughout the Western civilized world. On the other hand, there was clear evidence of emerging mutual unintelligibility among communities, with those who had once spoken Vulgar Latin in Portugal, Spain, France, Italy, Romania and elsewhere increasingly diverging from each other. There may even have been speculation about the future of Latin, given these already existing trends. Would the language fragment totally? Would Latin remain as a world lingua franca? Would there be anyone still learning the standard form in a thousand years? A millennium on, we know what happened. The standard forms of these languages are now indeed mutually unintelligible. Standard Latin is still used, but only by small numbers of clerics and scholars, chiefly within the Roman Catholic Church. A body of stalwart classicists, in universities and schools, try to maintain a tradition of Latin teaching, but do not find it easy. Latin, for most intents and purposes, is a dead language now. But its daughter-languages are very much alive.

Could this scenario happen to English? Certainly, there are some noteworthy parallels. English spread around the modern world in a time-frame not too dissimilar from that which must have affected Latin. Rome became a Republic in 509 BC, and the First Punic War (264–241 BC) resulted in the acquisition of its first overseas province, Sicily. Some two centuries later, Augustus established the Empire (31 BC), which lasted in the West until AD 476. So, basically, we are talking about a period of almost 1,000 years, with something like 750 years as the period of real expansion. Now consider English from the time of Bishop Aelfric – the first to put an English conversation down on paper (in his *Colloquy*, written around 1000). Another period of almost 1,000 years; and signs of language change very early on. During the eleventh century, a new variety of English began to develop in Scotland, much influenced by the refugees who had fled north in the years following the Norman Conquest; this Middle Scots was the basis of the very distinctive Scots English we know today. But the first overseas development was not until the end of the twelfth century, when English rule was imposed on Ireland by Henry II in 1171; the influence of Irish Gaelic on English must have been heard not long after. And from then until the twentieth century, covering the major period of English expansion around the world, we have – just like Latin – 750 years.

We can push the parallel a little further. What we consider to be the 'classics' of Latin literature – the 'Golden Age' of Augustus, with Ovid, Virgil, Horace, Livy *et al.* – emerged during the first century BC, some 400 years after the beginning of the Republic and some 200 years after the First Punic War. The first 'classic' of English literature, Chaucer's *Canterbury Tales*, was written some 400 years after our Y1K starting-point, and some 200 years after the Irish expedition. Let us move on another 200 years. This was a very significant century for both languages. During the third century AD the barbarian invasions began throughout Europe, becoming incessant in the next hundred years, and eventually leading to the decline of the Western Empire. Classical Latin became increasingly an elite language, and as lines of communication with Rome became more tenuous, so speech differences on the ground increased. Latin began its period of decline, as a spoken lingua franca. Another 200 years in England also brought a turning-point. We are now at the end of the sixteenth century. This was a time when the merits of English vs other languages, especially Latin, were being hotly debated, and there was much talk of decline. Richard Mulcaster, the headmaster of Merchant Taylors' School, was one of the strongest supporters of English, arguing for its strengths as a medium of educated expression, alongside Latin. But even he concluded that English could not compete with Latin as an international language. Writing in 1582, he says: 'Our English tongue is of small reach – it stretcheth no further than this island of ours – nay, not there over all.' And he reflects: 'Our state is no Empire to hope to enlarge it by commanding over countries.'[8] There was no real literature to be proud of, either, not since the time of 'Father Chaucer', as people would say, 200 years before – and Chaucer's English, because of the major pronunciation changes which had taken place in the early fifteenth century, had become virtually a different language.

1582. What a time to be saying such a thing. In the course of the next generation, things changed totally, both in politics and in literature. Within two years, Walter Raleigh's first expedition to America was to set sail, and although this was a failure, the first permanent English settlement was in place, in Jamestown, Virginia, a generation later. As we have seen, loan words from Indian languages into the English spoken there – which as a result started to turn into American English – become a significant feature of contemporary writing virtually immediately, and reference is soon being made to a distinctive American accent. And as for literature, 1582 was also significant, as it was the year in which a young man in Stratford, Warwickshire, fell in love – not with Gwyneth Paltrow (that came later), but with Anne Hathaway (his marriage licence is dated 27 November of that year). Soon after – we do not know how or when – he moved to London, and not long after that was being talked about as a writer. Within a generation, English literature would never be the same again.

Six hundred years into the spread of both Latin and English, there was a turning-point. In the case of Latin, it was the onset of fragmentation. In the case of English, it was the onset of expansion. Some 4–5 million people spoke English late in the reign of Queen Elizabeth I. This had grown to a quarter of the world's population, some 1.5 billion, late in the reign of Queen Elizabeth II. The contrast between Latin and English at this point seems total. But if history is any guide, it would appear that this period of expansion in English contained the seeds of its fragmentation. We do not talk about the 'Latin languages', but the 'Romance languages'. And, as we have seen, there is a book called *The English Languages*. History does seem to be repeating itself.

Centrifugal vs centripetal forces

However, history may no longer be a guide to what is happening to English today. The parallel with Latin is not perfect. One of the consequences of globalization is that through the media we have immediate access to other languages, and to varieties of English other than our own, in ways that have come to be available but recently; and this is altering the manner in which people are aware of the language. A British Council colleague told me recently that in India he had seen a group of people in an out-of-the-way village clustering around a television set, where they were hearing BBC News beamed down via satellite. None of these people, he felt, would have heard any kind of English before – at least, not in any regular or focused way – other than the Indian variety of English used by their school-teacher. But with a whole range of fresh auditory models becoming routinely available, it is easy to see how the type of English spoken in India could move in fresh directions. And satellite communication being, by definition, global, it is easy to see how a system of natural checks and balances – also well attested in the history of language – could emerge in the case of World English. In this scenario, the pull imposed by the need for identity, which has been making Indian English increasingly dissimilar from British English, is balanced by a pull imposed by the need for intelligibility, on a world scale, which will make Indian English increasingly similar. And this could happen anywhere.

Both centrifugal and centripetal forces operate on English. Alongside the need to reflect local situations and identities, which fosters diversity, there is the need for mutual comprehensibility, which fosters standardization. People need to be able to understand each other, both within a country and internationally. There has always been a need for lingua francas. And as supra-national organizations grow, the need becomes more pressing. The 191 members of the UN are there not simply to express their identities, but also because they want to talk to each other (at least, some of the time). And whatever languages are chosen by an organization as lingua francas, it is essential – if the concept is to work – for everyone to learn the same thing, a standard form of the language. In the case of English, when people get together on international occasions, or read the international press, or write books for international publication, what they use is Standard English.

In fact, Standard English isn't identical everywhere – the differences between British and American spelling are one obvious point – but it is very largely the same, especially in print. It is somewhat less established in speech, where differences will frequently be heard identifying people as British, American, Australian, and so on. However, these are still very few, and they may well diminish as international contacts increase. It is a cliché, but the world *has* become a smaller place, and this has an obvious linguistic consequence – that we talk to each other more, and come to understand each other more. British people can now watch American football on TV each week, and their awareness of that game's technical vocabulary increases as a result. A series on sumo wrestling on television a few years ago increased my knowledge of Japanese words in English tenfold. When we reflect on the opportunities for contact these days, the chances are that the standard element in international English will be strengthened. Satellite television, beaming down American and British English into homes all round the world, is a particularly significant development. An increasingly standardized spoken English is a likely outcome.

That is the reason why the history of Latin is no guide to the future of English. These centripetal forces were lacking a thousand years ago. Once the Roman Empire had begun to fragment, there was nothing to stop the centrifugal forces tearing spoken Latin apart. The numbers of Standard Latin speakers around Europe were small, and communication between groups was difficult. The whole globe now is communicatively smaller than Europe was then. It is the relative isolation of people from each other that causes a formerly common language to move in different directions. In the Middle Ages, it was very easy for communities to be isolated from the rest of the world. Today it is virtually impossible.

Both centrifugal and centripetal forces exist in the modern world, and we need both. We want to have our linguistic cake and to eat it. We want to express our identity through language and we want to communicate intelligibly through language. We want to be different and we want to be the same. And the splendid thing about humans using language, of course, is that this is perfectly possible. It is the kind of situation the multifunctional brain handles very well. We *can* have our cake and eat it. One of the main insights of twentieth-century linguistics was to demonstrate the extraordinary capacity of the brain for language. One of the consequences was the observation that bilingualism, multilingualism, is the *normal* human condition. Well over half of the people in the world, perhaps two-thirds, are bilingual. Children learn their languages – often several languages – at extraordinary speed. Evidently, there is something in our make-up which promotes the acquisition of speech. I therefore see no intrinsic problems in the gradual emergence of a tri-English world – a world, that is, in which a home dialect (often very mixed in character), a national standard dialect and an international standard dialect comfortably coexist. It is a prospect which our Latin forebears would have envied.

Let me illustrate the way three levels of English work from my own background:

- The base level, the place where we all start, is the home, our family dialect. In my case, this was Wales, and my home dialect was a Welsh English so strong in accent that when my family moved to Liverpool, when I was 10, I was immediately dubbed Taffy, and remained so even after my accent had moved in the direction of Liverpudlian. I am fluent today in both Welsh English and Scouse. I have two home dialects. Everybody has at least one.

- The second level is the national variety of Standard English which most people learn when they go to school. (With a minority of people, in the UK especially in South-east England, the home dialect is already Standard English.) In my case, this was British Standard English. I learned to write it, and gradually to speak it, avoiding such features as *ain't* and double negatives, and learning a different range of grammatical constructions and vocabulary than was found in my home dialect.

- The third level is an International Standard English – an English, in other words, which in its grammar and vocabulary is not recognizably British, American or anything else. When working abroad, many people become skilled in using a variety which lacks some of its original Britishness, because they know they are talking to people from outside the UK. International Standard Spoken English is not a global reality yet, but it is getting nearer.

Similar distinctions are to be found in other language settings too. Many foreign learners of English will have an ethnic or ancestral language for level one, and a national language for level two – such as (in Northern Spain) Basque for the first and Spanish for the second. The first two levels may also be very different forms of the same language, such as (in Southern Italy) Neapolitan and Standard Italian, respectively.

The new revolution

The twenty-first century is likely to see most educated first-language speakers of English becoming tri-dialectal –

triglossic is a term often used – whether in the UK, USA, Ghana, Singapore or anywhere that English has a significant national presence. Thanks to media exposure, these speakers are already tri-dialectal (at least) in their ability to comprehend regional varieties of English; and they will become increasingly tri-dialectal in their production too. Foreign-language learners will also find themselves needing to cope with these variations – developing a sense of international norms alongside the national norms which are currently the focus of teaching. Teachers already routinely draw attention to local lexical and grammatical differences, such as UK *pavement*, US *sidewalk* and Australian *footpath*, but the perspective is invariably from one of these varieties towards the others. Someone teaching British English draws attention to American alternatives, or vice versa. It may not be many years before an international standard will be the starting-point, with British, American and other varieties all seen as optional localizations.

I do not know how long it will take for such a scenario to become fully established. But I do know that it will not be an easy transition, as it will involve significant changes in our methods of teaching and examining. The situation is unprecedented, with more people using English in more places than at any time in the language's history, and unpredictable, with the forces promoting linguistic identity and intelligibility competing with each other in unexpected ways. For those who have to work professionally with English, accordingly, it is a very difficult time. After all, there has never been such a period of rapid and fundamental change since the explosions of development that hit the language in the Middle Ages and the Renaissance. For the first time in 400 years, we are experiencing what happens when English goes through a period of particularly dramatic change. It amounts to another revolution in the way the language is used – an exciting time to be a linguist, of course, to be in at the beginning of it, but a problematic time to be a teacher, having to guide others through it. Doubtless traditional practices in teaching language production will continue with little change for the time being, but there are already signs of a broadening of practice with respect to the teaching of listening comprehension. We are already living in a world where most of the varieties we encounter as we travel around the world are something other than traditional British or American English. Teachers do students a disservice if they let them leave their period of training unprepared for the brave new linguistic world which awaits them.

This chapter has focused on what is likely to happen to English as it copes with the pressures of becoming a global language in such a relatively short period of time. But there is another side to the coin. When a language becomes dominant within a country, there are always implications for other local languages: how do they maintain their identity? When a language becomes global, such implications affect all languages. A different set of questions arise as a consequence. Will the influence of English be so strong that it will permanently change the character of all other languages? And could English kill off other languages altogether? A world in which there was only one language left – an ecological intellectual disaster of unprecedented scale – is a scenario which could in theory obtain within 500 years. During the 1990s, people began to think seriously about such a possibility as a result of becoming aware of the second dimension to the language revolution.

2

The Future of Languages

No language exists in isolation. All languages in contact influence each other. Languages whose spread is widest – the leading international languages, such as French, Spanish, Chinese and Swahili – exercise most influence on their contact languages. And a global language, by its nature, exercises most influence of all.

One of the most notable trends of the last fifty years has been the way English, as it became increasingly global, began to affect the character of other languages through the arrival within them of unprecedented numbers of English loan words. Here are a dozen from the beginning of the alphabet, collected in Manfred Görlach's *Dictionary of European Anglicisms* (2001):

> AA ('Alcoholics Anonymous'), absenteeism, absorber (as in a fridge), abstract (content summary), accelerator, accountant, account executive, ace (tennis), acid (LSD), acid house (music), action film, AD ('art director')[1]

Cultures vary greatly in their response to this influx, and within each culture there are mixed attitudes. Some people welcome them, seeing them as a source of lexical enrichment; more puristically minded people condemn them, seeing them as an attack on traditional language values.

Organizations have been set up to fight them. In some famous cases, attempts have been made to ban them – the 1994 *loi Toubon* in France being perhaps the best-known instance. The energy and emotion generated has to be respected, but at the same time history tells us very firmly that it is misplaced. All languages have always been in contact with other languages. All languages have always borrowed words from other languages. And no language community has ever succeeded in stopping this process taking place. The only way to do so would be to take one's language away from contact with other languages. But no-one would want the social and economic isolationism that such a policy would imply.

There is a fallacy underlying the anti-borrowing position. Purists believe that borrowing words from other languages will lead to their own language changing its character and that this is a disaster. Change of character there certainly will be. Disaster there certainly won't be. The evidence, of course, comes from the history of languages, and especially from the history of English itself. A search through the *Oxford English Dictionary* shows that English over the centuries has borrowed words from over 350 other languages. As already pointed out in chapter 1, this has changed the character of English dramatically. Originally a Germanic language, English today is not like the English of Anglo-Saxon times: four-fifths of its vocabulary is not Germanic at all, in fact, but Romance, Latin or Greek. (I always find it ironic that when the French, for example, complain about the English words currently entering their language, they often end up objecting to words – a recent example is *le computer* – which have a French or Latin origin.)

English has undoubtedly changed, but has this been a bad thing? Much of the expressive impact of Chaucer and Shakespeare – to take just two of many authors – is due to their ability to work with all that multilingual vocabulary. And everyone benefits in a lexically enriched language. In English we have many 'doublets' and 'triplets', such as *kingly*, *royal* and *regal*, which stem from the borrowing history of the language – one Germanic, one French, one Latin. Three words for the same basic concept allows a whole range of stylistic nuances to be expressed which would not otherwise have been possible. Loan words always add semantic value to a language, giving people the opportunity to express their thoughts in a more nuanced way. And this is exactly what is happening in other languages at the moment: young people, for example, find many English loan words 'cool', in a way that the older generation does not, and their expressiveness is empowered as a consequence. The language as a whole thus acquires an extra lexical dimension which it did not have before. Many social domains now actively and creatively make use of English words – in advertising, for example, where the use of an English lexicon can actually help to sell goods. It is, of course, the same in English, but the other way round. French words in English help to sell perfume. And one of the most widely used expressions borrowed into British English via TV ads in the past decade or so has been *Vorsprung durch Technik*.

When a language adopts words – and also sounds and grammatical constructions – it adapts them. This is the repeated history of English, as it has spread around the world, evolving the New Englishes discussed in chapter 1, and a similar process will affect the loan words currently entering other languages too. When the French word *restaurant* entered English, it slowly changed its character, losing the French nasal vowel in the final syllable to end up first with 'rest-uh-rong' and eventually the modern pronunciation 'rest-ront'. Analogously, English words change their pronunciation, and eventually their English character, when they are re-pronounced in other languages. The syllabification which has affected English words entering Japanese is a well-studied case: several are now unintelligible to a native-English listener – which is one reason for the emergence of labels like 'Japlish', with the implication that these varieties are becoming new languages. Such labels are not jocular, as we have seen, though they are often used in that way: they are intuitive attempts to characterize what is happening linguistically around the world as languages become increasingly in contact with each other. They are a prime example of the point that human language cannot be controlled. The more a language becomes a national, then an international, then a global language, the more it ceases to be in the ownership of its originators. English itself has long since ceased to be owned by anyone, as we have seen, and is now open to the influence of all who choose to use it. That is why it is changing so much as it moves around the globe, and why the scenario of an English 'family of languages' is a major possibility for the twenty-first century.

The reason why vocabulary attracts all the attention is because the lexicon is the area where change is most rapid and noticeable. People are aware of new words, and new meanings of words. But not all borrowings attract the same amount of attention. Loan words tend to be of two types: words for concepts which the language never expressed before (as in much Internet vocabulary); and words for concepts which were already expressed by a perfectly satisfactory local word. It is this second category which receives criticism, because there is a fear that the new word will replace the old one. It is a misplaced fear, as I have suggested, for two reasons. First, as the many examples like *kingly* illustrate, the new word does not have to replace the old one, but can supplement it. As Spanish, for example, adopts English words, and adapts them, they cease to be English, and become Spanish – though conveying a different nuance alongside the traditional Spanish word. The process of integration is facilitated by many people, such as poets, novelists, dramatists, satirists, comedians, advertisers and journalists, who make use of these nuances creatively. It usually takes a generation for loan words to become integrated, though the Internet seems to be speeding up this time-frame. Looking back on previous generations' loan words, we value them, because we see the way that authors and others have made good use of them. It is only the current generation of borrowings that attracts criticism.

And second, even in cases where the new word does replace the old one (as often happened in English too, with hundreds of French words replacing Anglo-Saxon ones in the early Middle Ages), there is not very much that anyone can do about it. The point deserves repetition: human language cannot be controlled. A story is told by the twelfth-century historian Henry of Huntingdon that King Canute of England rebuked his flatterers by showing that even he, as king, could not stop the incoming tide – nor, by implication, the might of God. The story has great relevance when we think of individuals, societies, academies or even parliaments trying to stop the flow of loan words – whatever the language they are coming from. They have never managed it in the past. They never will in the future. Language is just too powerful, because too many speakers are involved. Apart from a handful of cases where the numbers of speakers are so few that their usage can be planned by a central body (as in the case of some endangered and minority languages), usage is beyond control. This is plainly the case with strong languages like French, Spanish and German, spoken in countries which have incorporated many ethnic identities.

Instead of attacking loan words, accordingly, it makes much more sense to develop creative strategies to foster their integration, in literature, school and society at large. That would be time and energy better spent. Loan words are the invisible exports of a world where people from different language backgrounds spend time with each other. They add new dimensions of linguistic life to a community. As a citizen of that world, I value every loan word I have in my linguistic repertoire, and look forward to the day when others feel the same. If people do have time and energy available to worry about linguistic matters, there are far more important issues deserving of their attention. Such as language death.

Languages in danger

Although languages have come into existence and died away throughout human history, it was only in the 1990s, following the publication of a series of worldwide surveys, that people began to notice that the rate of disappearance was significantly increasing.[2] The thrust of these facts is easy to summarize, even though it is impossible to be exact: of the 6,000 or so languages in the world, it seems probable that about half of these will disappear in the course of the present century – an average of one language dying out every two weeks or so. It is a rate of loss unprecedented in recorded history. Popular awareness of the facts is still very limited, and certainly nowhere near the corresponding awareness of biological loss that we associate with the environmental movement. Most people have yet to develop a language conscience. But the extent and rate of the ongoing loss in the world's linguistic diversity is currently so cataclysmic that it makes the word 'revolution' look like an understatement, when we consider it in this context.

Public interest in world language diversity is steadily growing, partly because the global story is being seen repeatedly in the histories of individual languages at risk, many of which are in Europe. Europe is fortunate in having several decades of experience in the management of minority languages, political and administrative structures to channel the expertise, and a history of decision-making which has resulted in important safeguards and recommendations. Indeed, several countries outside Europe look on the Continent's focus with great respect, and view with not a little envy situations like Welsh – where there are no fewer than two protective Language Acts already in place, and ongoing debate about a third. The local movements in support of Welsh, Gaelic, Catalan, Romansch and many other local languages have built up a dynamic which reached unprecedented levels in the 1990s, at least if judged by the number of public statements (such as the 1992 European Charter for Regional or Minority Languages and the 1996 Barcelona Declaration of Linguistic Rights).[3] International and national organizations concerned with language death (such as the UK's Foundation for Endangered Languages, or the UNESCO clearing-house at Tokyo) date from 1995. It is the recency of the movement which explains why it has so far had relatively little public presence, by comparison with the ecological movement in general, which has been gathering steam for half a century. But there is no doubt about the seriousness of the situation, which is proportionately much greater than in the case of zoological and botanical endangerment. Nobody is suggesting that half the world's species are going to die out in the next century.

The connection between the arrival of a global language (chapter 1) and the increased rate of language loss needs to be recognized, but not oversimplified. The impact of dominant languages on minority languages is a matter of universal concern, and the role of English is especially implicated. But it is important to stress that *all* majority languages are involved: the growth of English as a global language is not the sole factor in explaining language endangerment. Although it is English that has been the critical factor in the disappearance of languages in such parts of the world as Australia and North America, this language is of little relevance when we consider the corresponding losses that have taken place in South America or in many parts of Asia, where such languages as Spanish, Portuguese, Russian, Arabic and Chinese have replaced local languages. Nor, for that matter, is it always the chief factor in colonial Africa, where inter-ethnic and inter-religious rivalries at a local level are often the reason for the endangerment of a particular language. The thrust of the point is a general one: we are having to deal with the consequences of a globalization trend in which unprecedented market and cultural forces have been unleashed, steadily eroding the balance of linguistic power and involving all major languages.

A language dies when the last person who speaks it dies. Or, some people say, it dies when the second-last person who speaks it dies, for then the last person has nobody to talk to. A language lives on, after these deaths, only if it has been written down or recorded in some way. At the turn of the millennium, some 2,000 languages – about a third of the total – had still not been documented. When one of these languages disappears, the consequences are truly catastrophic. When people die, they leave signs of their presence in the world, in the form of their dwelling places, burial mounds and artefacts – in a word, their archaeology. But spoken language leaves no archaeology. When a language dies which has never been documented, it is as if it has never been.

It is the size of the problem which is so dramatic. There is of course nothing unusual about a single language dying. Communities have come and gone throughout history, and with them their language. Hittite, for example, died out when its civilization disappeared in Old Testament times, and some sixty languages known from biblical times shared the same fate. That is understandable. But what is happening today is extraordinary, judged by the standards of the past. Half the world's languages dying out within a century is language extinction on a massive and unprecedented scale. How do we know that so many languages will be lost? In the course of the past two or three decades, linguists all over the world have spent a great deal of time gathering comparative data. There have been several major surveys. And when people survey a language, they do not just make notes about its pronunciation, grammar and vocabulary, they also look at the number of people who speak it, and how old they are. Obviously, if they find a language with just a few speakers left, and nobody is bothering to pass the language on to the children, that language is bound to die out soon. And we have to draw the same conclusion if a language has fewer than 100 or 1,000 speakers. It is not likely to last very long.

In a survey which was published in 1999 by the US Summer Institute of Linguistics organization, Ethnologue, there were fifty-one languages with just one speaker left – twenty-eight of them in Australia alone. There were nearly 500 languages in the world with fewer than 100 speakers; 1,500 with fewer than 1000; over 3,000 with fewer than 10,000 speakers; and a staggering 5,000 languages with fewer than 100,000. It turns out that 96 per cent of the world's languages are spoken by just 4 per cent of the people. It is perhaps no wonder that so many are in danger.

The figure of 100,000, in the context of endangered languages, sometimes takes people by surprise. Surely a language with 100,000 speakers is safe? The evidence is to the contrary. Such a language is not going to die next week or next year; but there is no guarantee that it will still be surviving in a couple of generations. It all depends on the pressures being imposed upon it – in particular, whether it is at risk from the dominance of another language. It also depends on the attitudes of the people who speak it – do they care if it lives or dies? Breton, in North-west France, is a classic case of a language reducing dramatically in numbers. At the beginning of the twentieth century it was spoken by as many as a million people, but it is now down to less than a quarter of that total. Breton could be saved if enough effort is made – the kind of effort that has already helped Welsh to recover its growth – and there are signs of this happening. If not, the downward trend will just continue, and it could be gone in fifty years. This scenario has already happened, in recent times, to two other Celtic languages in North-western Europe – Cornish, formerly spoken in Cornwall, and Manx, in the Isle of Man. Both are currently attracting support, in an effort to restore what has been lost; but once a language has lost its last community of native speakers, the task of resurrecting it – although not impossible, as has been seen with some of the Aboriginal languages of Australia – is hugely difficult.

It does not take a language long to disappear, once the will to continue with it leaves its community. In fact, the speed of decline has been one of the main findings of recent linguistic research. An example is Aleut, the language of the Aleutian Islands west of Alaska, surviving mainly in just one village, Atka. In 1990 there were sixty fluent speakers left; by 1994 there were just forty-four. If that rate of decline continues, Aleut will effectively be gone by 2010. Given the age of the youngest speakers, still in their twenties, it will probably live on until the middle of the century, spoken sporadically, until eventually those last few speakers, isolated from each other and lacking the opportunities to renew their language through daily inter- action, find they have no-one to talk to. This is a scenario that can be encountered anywhere in the world, but espe- cially in the regions close to the Equator – in Brazil, West Africa, India and South-east Asia (especially Papua New Guinea) – where the majority of the world's languages are spoken.

Why are so many languages dying? The reasons range from natural disasters, through different forms of cultural assimilation, to genocide. Consider the first factor. Though accurate figures are virtually impossible to come by, it is evident that small communities in isolated areas can easily be decimated or wiped out by earthquakes, hurricanes, tsunamis and other cataclysms. On 17 July 1998, a 7.1 magnitude earthquake off the coast of East Saundaun Pro- vince, Papua New Guinea, killed over 2,200 and displaced over 10,000: the villages of Sissano, Warupu, Arop and Malol were destroyed; some 30 per cent of the Arop and Warupu villagers were killed. The people in these vil- lages had already been identified by Summer Institute of Linguistics researchers as being sufficiently different from each other in their speech to justify the recognition of four separate languages, but the matter was unresolved: according to Ethnologue (1996), surveys were needed in three cases; some work was in progress in the fourth. The numbers were already small: Sissano had only 4,776 inhabitants in the 1990 census; Malol was estimated to have 3,330; Arop 1,700 in 1981; and Warupu 1,602 in 1983. The totals for Arop and Warupu will now each be at least 500 fewer. But as the villages were destroyed, and the survivors moved away to care centres and other locations, there must now be a real question-mark over whether these communities (and thus their languages) will survive the trauma of displacement.

The historical effect of imported disease on indigenous peoples is well established, though the extraordinary scale of the effects in the early colonial period is still not widely appreciated. Within 200 years of the arrival of the first Europeans in the Americas, it is thought that over 90 per cent of the indigenous population was killed by the diseases which accompanied them, brought in by both animals and humans. To take just one area: the Central Mexico population is believed to have been something over 25 million in 1518, when the Spanish arrived, but it had dropped to 1.6 million by 1620. Some estimates suggest that the population of the New World may have been as high as 100 million before European contact. Within 200 years this had dropped to fewer than 1 million. The scale of this disaster can only be appreciated by comparing it with others: it far exceeds the 25 million thought to have died from the Black Death in fourteenth-century Europe; it even well exceeds the combined total of deaths in the two World Wars (some 30–40 million). Smallpox then; AIDS today. But diseases such as influenza and measles can just as easily be killers in a community that has no immunity to them, as has been repeatedly seen among the Amerindian languages of South America.

In parts of the world where indigenous natural resources have been subject to outside exploitation, the effect on the local people has been devastating, as is regularly documented by human rights organizations. The treatment of the communities of the Amazonian rainforest continues to provide cause for international condemnation. Despite decades of effort to secure land rights for the indigenous peoples, and to give them protection against the aggression of ranchers, miners and loggers, reports of ethnic murder and displacement are still common. In other parts of the world, it is the political, rather than the economic, situation in a country which is the immediate cause of the decimation or disappearance of a community. The damage may be the result of civil war, or of conflict on an international scale. Long-standing ethnic or religious enmities may be implicated, as in parts of Africa. Claims about genocide are common.

In many places, it is difficult to disentangle political and economic factors. The disappearance of several languages in Colombia, for example, has been attributed to a mixture of aggressive circumstances. One strand highlights a history of military conflict, in which several indigenous communities have been exterminated. The conflict is complex, involving regular, paramilitary, guerrilla and criminal (drug-related) forces operating in rural areas; members of ethnic communities find themselves embroiled in the conflicts, often suspected by one of these forces as acting as collaborators with the other(s). Another strand highlights the exploitation of small communities by organizations both from within the country and from outside, with reported instances of slave labour (for rubber production along the Amazon) and of forced migrations from rural areas to the cities. Whatever the balance of causes, the result has been the same – significant mortality of the people, and short-term community disintegration.

The people may live, but the language may still die. The remaining cluster of factors causing language loss has nothing directly to do with the physical safety of a people. The members of the community remain alive and well, often continuing to inhabit their traditional territory; but their language nonetheless goes into decline, and eventually disappears, to be replaced by some other language. The term most often encountered in this connection is *cultural assimilation*: one culture is influenced by a more dominant culture, and begins to lose its character as a result of its members adopting new behaviour and mores. Much of the present crisis stems from the major cultural movements which began 500 years ago, as colonialism spread a small number of dominant languages around the world. The point hardly needs to be stressed in such places as North America and Australia, where English has displaced so many aboriginal languages – but, as already mentioned, we must not forget that English is by no means the only language which has dominated in this way. In South America, it was Spanish and Portuguese. In northern Asia, it was Russian. Nor has European colonialism been the only cause. Arabic has steamrollered many languages in northern Africa. And in sub-Saharan Africa, local tribal empire-building has always been a critical factor.

Today, the factors which foster cultural assimilation are well known. Urbanization has produced cities which act as magnets to rural communities, and developments in transport and communications have made it easier for country people to reach them. Within these cities they have immediate access to the consumer society, with its specifically American biases, and the homogenization which contact of this kind inevitably brings. The learning of a dominant language – such as Spanish or Portuguese in South America, Swahili in much of East Africa, Arabic in North Africa, and English virtually everywhere – immensely facilitates this process. Even if people stay in their rural setting, there is no escape (except for the most isolated communities), because the same transport systems which carry country people into the cities are used to convey consumer products and the associated advertising back to their communities. The centralization of power within the metropolis invariably results in a loss of autonomy for local communities, and often a sense of alienation as they realize that they are no longer in control over their own destinies, and that local needs are being disregarded by distant decision-makers. The language of the dominant culture infiltrates everywhere, reinforced by the relentless daily pressure of the media, and especially of television. Traditional knowledge and practices are quickly eroded.

When one culture assimilates to another, the sequence of events affecting the endangered language seems to be the same everywhere. There are three broad stages. The first is immense pressure on the people to speak the dominant language – pressure that can come from political, social or economic sources. It might be 'top-down', in the form of incentives, recommendations or laws introduced by a government or national body; or it might be 'bottom-up', in the form of fashionable trends or peer group pressures from within the society of which they form a part; or again, it might have no clear direction, emerging as the result of an interaction between sociopolitical and socioeconomic factors that are only partly recognized and understood. But wherever the pressure has come from, the result – stage two – is a period of emerging bilingualism, as people become increasingly efficient in their new language while still retaining competence in their old. Then, often quite quickly, this bilingualism starts to decline, with the old language giving way to the new. This leads to the third stage, in which the younger generation becomes increasingly proficient in the new language, identifying more with it, and finding their first language less relevant to their new needs. This is often accompanied by a feeling of shame about using the old language, on the part of the parents as well as their children. Parents use the old language less and less to their children, or in front of their children; and when more children come to be born within the new society, they find fewer opportunities to use that language to them. Those families which do continue to use the language find there are fewer other families to talk to, and their own usage becomes inward-looking and idiosyncratic, resulting in 'family dialects'. Outside the home, the children stop talking to each other in the language. Within a generation – sometimes even within a decade – a healthy bilingualism within a family can slip into a self-conscious semilingualism, and thence into a monolingualism which places that language one step nearer to extinction.

The twenty-first-century challenge: documentation and revitalization

Can anything be done? Obviously it is too late to do anything to help many languages, where the speakers are too few or too old, and where the community is too busy just trying to survive to care about its language. But many other languages are not in such a serious position. Often, where languages are endangered, there are things that can be done to give new life to them. The term is *revitalization*. A community, once it realizes that its language is in danger, can get its act together, and introduce measures which can genuinely revitalize it. There are successful and well-publicized examples in Australia and North America. Within the British Isles, the most successful instance of a revitalized language is Welsh. Everything has to be right, of course, for there to be a likelihood of success. The community itself must want to save its language. The culture of which it is a part must need to have a respect for minority languages. There needs to be funding, to enable courses, materials and teachers to be introduced. And, in a huge number of cases, there need to be linguists, to get on with the basic task of putting the language down on paper, or in its digital equivalent.

That is the main task: getting the language documented – recorded, analysed, written down. There are two reasons for this. The obvious one is educational – the need for literacy. But there is a second reason, and this is all to do with why we should care about dying languages in the first place. We should care for the very same reason that we care when a species of animal or plant dies. It reduces the diversity of our planet. We are talking about intellectual and cultural diversity now, of course, not biological diversity; but the issues are the same. Most people would accept without need for argument the proposition that biodiversity is a good thing, and that its preservation should be fostered. Following decades of green publicity and activism, they are now aware. Linguistic diversity, unfortunately, has not had the same press. People, on the whole, are not aware. What might be done to improve public awareness is discussed further in chapter 4.

Diversity has a central place in evolutionary thought, where it is seen as the result of species genetically adapting in order to survive in different environments. Increasing uniformity holds dangers for the long-term survival of a species. The strongest ecosystems are those which are most diverse. And, in its application to human development, the point has often been made that our success in colonizing the planet has been due to our ability to develop diverse cultures which suit all kinds of environments. The need to maintain linguistic diversity stands squarely on the shoulders of such arguments. If diversity is a prerequisite for successful humanity, then the preservation of linguistic diversity is essential, for language lies at the heart of what it means to be human. If the development of multiple cultures is so important, then the role of languages becomes critical, for cultures are chiefly transmitted through spoken and written languages. Encapsulated within a language is most of a community's history, and a large part of its cultural identity. 'Every language is a temple', said Oliver Wendell Holmes, 'in which the soul of those who speak it is enshrined.'[4] And if the amount of diversity is a critical factor, then the more languages we can preserve the better.

The world is a mosaic of visions. We learn so much from the visions of others, and to lose even one piece of this mosaic is a loss for all of us. Sometimes the learning is eminently practical, as when we discover new medical treatments from the folk medicine practices of an indigenous people. Sometimes it is intellectual – an increase in our awareness of the history of our world, as when the links between languages tell us something about the movements of early civilizations. 'I am always sorry when any language is lost,' said Dr Johnson, 'because languages are the pedigree of nations.'[5] Sometimes it is literary: every language has its equivalent – even if only in oral form – of Chaucer, Wordsworth and Dickens. And of course, very often it is linguistic: we learn something new about language itself – the behaviour that makes us truly human. Ezra Pound summed up the core intellectual argument: 'The sum of human wisdom is not contained in any one language, and no single language is capable of expressing all forms and degrees of human comprehension.'[6] And for the complementary perspective, we can turn to George Steiner: 'Is it not the duty of the critic to avail himself, in some imperfect measure at least, of another language – if only to experience the defining contours of his own?'[7]

There are, accordingly, good ecological, social and linguistic reasons why we should care about language death, and get on with the task of documenting endangered languages as quickly as possible. With every language that dies, another precious source of data about the nature of the human language faculty is lost – and we must not forget that there are only about 6,000 sources in all. But nonetheless, not everyone believes in the value of a multilingual world. Some deep-rooted myths exist. The worst is the Babel myth: people think that the multiplicity of the world's languages is a curse rather than a blessing, imposed by God as a punishment for the overweening pride of humanity. This argument runs: if only we had just one language in the world – whether English, Esperanto or whatever – we would all be better off. There would be no misunderstanding. It would be a new reign of world peace.

The argument sounds very attractive; but it is nonsense. It is nothing to do with whether you believe in the Bible or not. Let us leave aside the question of whether there ever was a single language pre-Babel. (Genesis 10 suggests there was not, as it lists the sons of Japheth 'according to their countries and each of their languages' – well before the Babel event, which is not reported until Genesis 11.) The fact of the matter is that a monolingual world would not bring peace in the future any more than is found within monolingual countries today. Quite the contrary. It is interesting how many of the really big trouble spots of the world in recent decades have been countries characterized by their monolingualism, such as Cambodia, Vietnam, Rwanda and Burundi – the latter two pre-eminent in Africa in this regard – and the Serbo-Croatian-speaking sector of former Yugoslavia. Northern Ireland, too, if you will. And all major monolingual countries have had their civil wars. If people want to fight each other, it seems that it takes more than a common language to stop them.

We are far more likely to promote a peaceful world by paying attention to people's rights and to their identities as communities – and the chief emblem, or badge, of a community is its language. A sensitive policy of multilingualism, and a concern for minority languages, is much more likely to lay the foundation for peaceful and mutually beneficial coexistence. And we develop such a policy only by becoming aware, genuinely aware, of the benefits of bilingualism – a principle which the leading nations, largely monolingual by historical temperament, are still having some difficulty taking on board. They need to reflect on Emerson's words: 'As many languages as he has, as many friends, as many arts and trades, so many times is he a man.'[8] Or the Slovakian proverb: 'With each newly learned language you acquire a new soul.'

Of course, in some parts of the world, all this talk of language must be put in a broader perspective. It is axiomatic that physical wellbeing is a top priority: there is no point in going on to people about language if they are too ill to speak or too hungry to listen. If food, welfare and work are lacking, then it is only to be expected that they will direct their energies to ways of increasing resources and fostering economic growth. The same applies if military conflict, political oppression or civil disturbance threaten daily safety and survival. Language preservation then almost seems like an irrelevant luxury. And yet, it is a fact of life that circumstances, priorities and goals all change with time. If the development programmes fostered by international organizations are at all successful, then the hope is that there will come a time when, healthy and well fed, people will have the time and energy to devote to quality, as opposed to quantity, of life. At that point, they will look to revive their cultural traditions and to affirm their cultural identity. That is when they will look for their language.

One of the loudest complaints to eventually emerge is of the 'if only' type: 'if only my parents had . . . '; 'if only my grandparents' generation had . . . '. This kind of reaction is very common among the members of a community two generations after the one which failed to pass its language on. The first generation is typically not so concerned, as its members are often still struggling to establish their new social position and new language. It is their children,

The Future of Languages

secure in the new language and in a much better socio-economic state, with battles over land-claims and civil rights behind them, who begin to reflect on the heritage they have lost, and to wish that things had been otherwise. The 'old language', formerly a source of shame, comes to be seen as a source of identity and pride. But by then, without any preservation measures, it is too late. If their language has gone, unrecorded and unremembered, there is no way in which they can get it back. By contrast, if a modicum of effort has been devoted to language preservation, even in the most difficult of economic circumstances, at least these people have kept their options open. They can make their choice, whether we are thinking about this generation, or a generation ahead.

A modicum of effort. This is the twenty-first-century challenge. Could we save a few thousand languages, just like that? Of course, if the will and funding were available. So how much would it cost? It is not cheap, when you think of what has to be done – getting linguists into the field, supporting the community with language resources and teachers, publishing grammars and dictionaries, writing materials for use in schools – and all over a period of several years, because it takes time to revitalize an endangered language. Conditions vary so much that it is difficult to generalize, but a figure of £100,000 a year per language would enable a great deal to be done. If we devoted that amount of effort over three years for each of 3,000 languages, we would be talking about some £900 million to have a real impact on the present crisis. Whether we talk in pounds or dollars, that sounds like a lot. But let us put it in perspective. It is equivalent to a couple of days' oil revenues, in an average year. Three thousand languages documented and their revitalization initiated for around a billion pounds/dollars? Where else would you get such value for money?

The process has begun, slowly and with difficulty. During the 1990s, several organizations were established to try to channel the energies involved, and to raise funds. I have already mentioned the Foundation for Endangered Languages started in the UK in 1995, and there are similar organizations in the USA, Germany, Japan and elsewhere. The UNESCO initiative which commenced in the same year was taken further by a fresh statement in March 2003 reflecting the urgency of the situation.[9] There is, it seems, no shortage of applicants willing to 'get out there' and work on these languages. In many localities, there are already several well-trained indigenous people already 'out there'. The problem in all cases is funding. The need is obvious, but needs are met only through con- sciousness raising, using academic writing, broadcasting, journalism and as many channels of communication as possible – not least, as I shall argue in chapter 4, the arts. Getting a sense of 'red alert' into the public mind, on a global scale, is probably the most critical linguistic initia- tive which has to be taken in the new millennium. A decade ago, it would have been very difficult to see how this might be done. Today, a number of avenues have opened up, largely due to the opportunities provided by the third feature of the language revolution – the Internet.

3

The Role of the Internet

The public acquisition of the Internet was the third element contributing to the revolutionary linguistic character of the 1990s, and the one where the epithet 'revolutionary' is easiest to justify. Although the Internet as a technology had been around since the 1960s, for e-mails and chat, very few people began exploiting it until thirty years later. The World Wide Web itself came into existence only in 1991. But in an extraordinarily short time, people adopted and mastered the technology, and in the course of doing that encountered, adapted and expanded its highly distinctive language. To begin with, people found the linguistic novelty to lie chiefly in the slang and jargon of its enthusiastic proponents, as well as in their penchant for playing with language and for breaking conventional linguistic rules of spelling and punctuation. Linguists were especially impressed by the speed with which linguistic innovation could be circulated worldwide. But gradually, it became apparent that the Internet was manifesting more than a new stylistic variety of a language. It was providing us with a further alternative to the mediums through which human communication can take place. This alternative is so new that it still has no generally agreed name – *computer-mediated communication* (CMC) and *electronic communication* are two which have been suggested – nor is there an accepted term for the kind of language it manifests (the term I use is *Netspeak*).[1] But there are good grounds for viewing the arrival of the Internet as an event which is as revolutionary in linguistic terms as it has been technologically and socially.

Revolutions of this order of magnitude are rare events indeed. The first medium of communication was, of course, speech, which emerged in the human race somewhere between 30,000 and 100,000 years ago. Then, some 10,000 years ago, in several parts of the world, we encounter the emergence of writing. Those two mediums have kept the human race satisfactorily communicating ever since, each facilitated from time to time by the arrival of new technology – notably telephony and broadcasting, in the case of speech, and printing and telegraphy, in the case of writing. We must also acknowledge the significance of a third medium of communication for an important section of society – deaf sign language, which has an obscure history until it began to be systematically recorded in the eighteenth century, and which exists today in a number of forms. But a new medium of communication affecting the whole of society has not appeared in 10,000 years.

What are the grounds for talking in such a revolutionary tone? Why am I not content to describe computer-mediated communication in traditional terms – simply as 'written language on screen'? The answer can be seen in the struggle commentators have had to describe exactly what is happening when people communicate in this way. E-mails, for example, have been called 'written speech', 'a cross between a conversation and a letter', and 'a strange blend of writing and talking'.[2] When Homer Simpson asks his friends 'What's an e-mail?', they scratch their heads. Lenny replies: 'It's a computer thing, like, er, an electric letter.' Carl adds: 'Or a quiet phone call.'[3] And when we take the other functions of the Internet into account, the difficulty of arriving at a simple characterization in terms of traditional speech or writing becomes even greater. Some commentators have likened the Internet to an amalgam of television, telephone and conventional publishing, and the term *cyberspace* has been coined to capture the notion of a world of information present or possible in digital form (earlier called the *information superhighway*).

To appreciate the novelty of the medium, we need to consider all the functions that it is capable of performing. In the final analysis, the Internet is no more than an association of computer networks with common standards which enable messages to be sent from any central computer (or *host*) on one network to any host on any other. However, it is now the world's largest computer network, with over 100 million hosts connected by the year 2000, providing an increasing range of services and enabling unprecedented numbers of people to be in touch with each other through a variety of techniques. Three broad functions can be identified:

1 The *World Wide Web* (or *Web*) is the most widely encountered manifestation of this network – the full collection of all the computers linked to the Internet which hold documents that are mutually accessible through the use of a standard protocol (the HyperText Transfer Protocol, or HTTP). The creator of the Web, computer scientist Tim Berners-Lee, has defined it as 'the universe of network-accessible information, an embodiment of human knowledge'.[4] It was devised in 1990 as a means of enabling high-energy physicists in different institutions to share information within their field, but it rapidly spread to other fields, and is now all-inclusive in subject-matter, designed for multimedia interaction between computer users anywhere in the world. Its many functions include encyclopedic reference, archiving, cataloguing, 'Yellow Pages' listing, advertising, self-publishing, games, news

reporting, creative writing and commercial transactions of all kinds, with movies and other types of entertainment becoming increasingly available.

2 *Electronic mail* (or *e-mail*) is the use of computer systems to transfer messages between users – now chiefly used to refer to messages sent between private mailboxes (as opposed to those posted to a chatgroup). Although it takes up only a relatively small domain of Internet 'space', by comparison with the billions of pages on the Web, it far exceeds the Web in terms of the number of daily individual transactions made. As John Naughton has said, 'The Net was built on electronic mail. ... It's the oil which lubricates the system.'[5] It is extremely diverse in character, comprising personal and institutional messages of varying length and purpose.

3 *Chatgroups* are continuous discussions on a particular topic, organized in 'rooms' at particular Internet sites, in which computer users interested in the topic can participate. There are two types of situation, depending on whether the interaction takes place in real time (*synchronous*) or in postponed time (*asynchronous*). In a synchronous situation, a user enters a chatroom and joins an ongoing conversation in real time, sending named contributions which are inserted into a permanently scrolling screen along with the contributions from other participants. In an asynchronous situation, the interactions are stored in some format and made available to users upon demand, so that they can catch up with the discussion, or add to it, at any time – even after an appreciable period has passed. A distinctive use of this technology takes the form of 'multi-user domains' – imaginary environments where people can play text-based fantasy games (of the 'dungeons and dragons' type) or construct virtual worlds (e.g. in business or education) where they can simulate real-life situations and engage in various role-playing scenarios.

These three situations are not mutually exclusive. It is possible to find sites in which all are combined, or where one situation is used within another. For example, many Web sites contain discussion groups and e-mail links; e-mails often contain Web attachments. The Internet world is an extremely fluid one, with users exploring its possibilities of expression, introducing fresh combinations of elements, and reacting to technological developments. But one thing is plain. These three functions, in their different ways, facilitate and constrain our ability to communicate in ways that are fundamentally different from those found in other semiotic situations. Many of the expectations and practices which we associate with spoken and written language no longer obtain, and new opportunities arise. As a consequence, people find they have to get to grips with the communicative potential made available to them – and here they encounter a problem. They have to learn the rules – of how to communicate via e-mail, of how to socialize in chatgroups, of how to construct an effective Web page – and yet there are no rules, in the sense of universally agreed modes of behaviour established by generations of usage. This is a clear contrast with the world of paper-based communication. Letter-writing, for instance, is routinely taught in school; and because there is widespread agreement on how letters are to be written, supported by the recommendations of usage manuals, we feel secure in that knowledge. But no such agreed guide to usage yet exists in the case of Netspeak. Before too long, Netspeak conventions will come to be routinely taught in schools. In the meantime, often the first indication that we have misconstructed a message comes when we receive an unpalatable response from our recipient.

The Internet is an electronic, global and interactive medium, and each of these properties has consequences for the kind of language found there. The most fundamental influence arises out of the electronic character of the channel. Most obviously, a user's communicative options are constrained by the nature of the hardware needed in order to gain Internet access. Thus, a set of characters on a keyboard determines productive linguistic capacity (the type of information that can be sent); and the size and configuration of the screen determines receptive linguistic capacity (the type of information that can be seen). Both sender and receiver are additionally constrained linguistically by the properties of the Internet software and hardware linking them. There are, accordingly, certain traditional linguistic activities that this medium can facilitate very well, and others that it cannot handle at all. There are also certain linguistic activities which an electronic medium allows that no other medium can achieve. That is why it seems apposite to talk in terms of 'revolution'.

Not like speech

Computer-mediated communication is not like speech, even in those electronic situations which are most speech-like, such as e-mailing. There are several major differences between CMC and face-to-face conversation. The first is a function of the technology – the lack of simultaneous feedback. The success of a conversation totally depends on the participants providing each other with immediate feedback. While you speak to me, I do not stay unmoved and silent: my face and voice provide an ongoing commentary on what you are saying. Nods and smiles work along with a wide range of vocalizations, such as *uh-huh*, *yeah*, *sure* and *ooh*. Such messages from our listeners tell us how we are doing, and we react to them instinctively and immediately. A puzzled look makes us rephrase.

A doubtful *hmm* makes us rethink. Without these, a conversation quickly breaks down, or becomes extremely stilted and artificial. It is difficult enough on the telephone, when just the visual cues are absent. Imagine the difficulty in a face-to-face conversation if both visual and auditory feedback were missing.

But that is how it is in e-mail and chatgroup interaction. Messages sent via a computer are complete and unidirectional. When we send a message to someone, we type it a keystroke at a time, but it does not arrive on that person's screen a keystroke at a time – in the manner of the old teleprinters. The message does not leave our computer until we 'send' it, and that means the whole of a message is transmitted as a unit, and arrives on the recipient's screen as a unit. There is no way that a recipient can react to our message while it is being typed, for the obvious reason that recipients do not know they are getting any messages at all until the text arrives. Correspondingly, there is no way for a sender to get a sense of how successful a message is while it is being written – whether it has been understood, or whether it needs repair. There is no technical way (at the moment) which would allow the receiver to send the electronic equivalent of a simultaneous nod, an *uh-uh*, or any of the other audio-visual reactions which play such a critical role in face-to-face interaction. Messages cannot overlap. As a result, recipients are committed to experiencing a waiting period before the text appears – on their screen there is nothing, and then there is something, an 'off–on' system which well suits the binary computer world but which is far removed from the complex realities of everyday conversation. This factor alone makes e-conversations totally unlike those which take place in 'real world' speech.

The second big difference between Netspeak and face-to-face conversation can be illustrated from real-time chatrooms. If you are in a chatroom, talking around a particular theme, you see on your screen messages coming in from all over the world. If there are thirty people in the room, then you could be seeing up to thirty different messages, all making various contributions to the theme, but often clustering into half a dozen or so sub-conversations. It is a bit like being in a cocktail party where there are other conversations going on all around you. In the party, of course, you can't pay attention to all of them or contribute to all of them at the same time. In a chatroom you can't avoid attending to them, and you can contribute to as many as your mental powers and typing speed permit. It has never been possible before, in the history of human communication, to participate simultaneously in multiple conversations. Now you can. This too is a revolutionary state of affairs, as far as speech is concerned.

A third difference results from the temporal limitations of the technology: the rhythm of an Internet interaction is very much slower than that found in a speech situation, and disallows some of conversation's most salient properties. With e-mails and asynchronous chatgroups, a response to a stimulus may be anything from seconds to months, the rhythm of the exchange very much depending on such factors as the recipient's computer (e.g. whether it announces the instant arrival of a message), the user's personality and habits (e.g. whether messages are replied to at regular times or randomly) and the circumstances of the interlocutors (e.g. their computer access). The time-delay (usually referred to as *lag*) is a central factor in many situations: there is an inherent uncertainty in knowing the length of the gap between the moment of posting a message and the moment of receiving a reaction. Because of lag, the rhythm of an interaction – even in the fastest Netspeak encounters – lacks the pace and predictability of that found in telephonic or face-to-face conversation.

Even if a participant types a reply immediately, there may be a delay before that message reaches the other members' screens, due to several factors, such as bandwidth processing problems, traffic density on the host computer, or some problem in the sender's or receiver's equipment.

Lag problems make chatroom interactions very different from anything humans have experienced in dialogue before. The frustration is on both sides of the communication chain. From the sender's point of view, the right moment to speak may be missed, as the point to which the intended contribution related may have scrolled off the screen and be fast receding from the group's communal memory. And from the recipient's point of view, the lack of an expected reaction is ambiguous, as there is no way of knowing whether the delay is due to transmission reasons or to some 'attitude' on the sender's part. Unexpected silence in a telephone conversation carries a similar ambiguity, but at least there we have well-established turn-taking manoeuvres which can bring immediate clarification ('Hello?', 'Are you still there?'). The linguistic strategies which express our face-to-face conversational exchanges are much less reliable in chatgroups. Colin may never get a reaction to his reply to Jane because Jane may never have received it (for technical reasons), may not have noticed it (because there are so many other remarks coming in at the same time), may have been distracted by some other conversation (real or on-line), may not have been present at her terminal to see the message (for all kinds of reasons), or simply decided not to respond. Equally, she may have replied, and it is *her* message which has got delayed or lost. When responses are disrupted by delays, there is little anyone can do to sort such things out.

The larger the number of participants involved in an interaction, the worse the situation becomes. Delays in a

conversation between two people are annoying and ambiguous, but the level of disruption is usually manageable,
because each person has only one interlocutor to worry
about. If a simple e-mail situation is affected by serious
delay, feedback via phone or fax is easily providable. But
when an electronic interaction involves several people, such
as in chatgroups, virtual worlds and e-mails which are
copied repeatedly, lag produces a very different situation,
because it interferes with another core feature of traditional
face-to-face interaction: the conversational *turn*. Turn-
taking is so fundamental to conversation that most people
are not conscious of its significance as a means of enabling
interactions to be successful. But it is a conversational fact
of life that people follow the routine of taking turns when
they talk, and avoid talking at once or interrupting each
other randomly or excessively. Moreover, they expect certain 'adjacency-pairs' to take place: questions to be followed
by answers, and not the other way round; similarly, a piece
of information to be followed by an acknowledgement, or a
complaint to be followed by an excuse or apology. These
elementary strategies, learned at a very early age, provide
a normal conversation with its skeleton.

When there are long lags, the conversational situation
becomes so unusual that its ability to cope with a topic can
be destroyed. This is because the turn-taking, as seen on a
screen, is dictated by the software, and not by the participants: in a chatgroup, for instance, even if we did start to
send a reaction to someone else's utterance before it was
finished, the reaction would take its turn in a non-overlap-
ping series of utterances on the screen, dependent only on
the point at which the send signal was received at the host
server. Messages are posted to a receiver's screen linearly,
in the order in which they are received by the system. In
a multi-user environment, messages are coming in from
various sources all the time, and with different lags.

Because of the way packets of information are sent electronically through different global routes between sender and receiver, it is even possible for turn-taking reversals to take place, and all kinds of unpredictable overlaps. The time-frames of the participants do not coincide. Lucy asks a question; Sue receives it and sends an answer; but on Ben's screen the answer is received before the question. Or, Lucy sends a question, Sue replies, and Lucy sends another question; but on Ben's screen the second question arrives before Sue's reply to the first. The situation may be further complicated if Sue (or anyone) decides to answer two questions from different participants, sending them together. Steve, meanwhile, copied in to the exchanges, is out of the office, and responds a day later, after other messages have come in. There are enormous possibilities for confusion once orderly turn-taking is so disruptable and adjacency-pairs are so interruptible. What is surprising is that practised participants seem to tolerate (indeed revel in) the anarchy which ensues.

Issues of feedback and turn-taking are ways in which computer-mediated interaction differs from conversational speech. But it is unlike speech also with respect to the formal properties of the medium – properties that are so basic that it becomes extremely difficult for people to live up to the recommendation that they should 'write as they talk'. Chief among these properties is the domain of *tone of voice* – 'it ain't what you say but the way that you say it' – as expressed through vocal variations in pitch (intonation), loudness (stress), speed, rhythm, pause and other vocal effects. There have been somewhat desperate efforts to replace tone of voice on screen in the form of an exaggerated use of spelling and punctuation, and the use of capitals, spacing and special symbols for emphasis. Examples include repeated letters (*aaaaahhhhh*, *soooo*), repeated punctuation marks (*whohe????*, *hey!!!*), and conventions for expressing emphasis, such as *the *real* point.* These features are capable of a certain expressiveness, but the range of meanings they signal are few, and restricted to gross notions such as extra emphasis, surprise and puzzlement. Less exaggerated nuances are not capable of being handled in this way.

Related to this is the way Netspeak lacks the facial expressions, gestures and conventions of body posture which are so critical in expressing personal opinions and attitudes and in moderating social relationships. The limitation was noted early in the development of Netspeak, and led to the introduction of *smileys* or *emoticons* – combinations of keyboard characters designed to show an emotional facial expression. The two basic types express positive attitudes and negative attitudes respectively (the omission of the 'nose' element seems to be solely a function of typing speed or personal taste):

:-) or :)   :-(or : (

Hundreds of ludic shapes and sequences have been invented and collected in smiley dictionaries, some extremely ingenious and artistic, but hardly any are used in serious communication. It is plain that they are a potentially helpful but very crude way of capturing some of the basic features of facial expression. They can forestall a gross misperception of a speaker's intent, but an individual smiley still allows a huge number of readings (happiness, joke, sympathy, good mood, delight, amusement, etc.) which can be disambiguated only by referring to the verbal context. Without care, moreover, they can lead to their own misunderstanding: adding a smile to an utterance which is plainly angry can increase rather than decrease the force of the 'flame'. It is a common experience that a smile can go down the wrong way.

The fact that smileys turn up at all in e-mails and chat-room interaction is indicative of the un-speech-like nature of the medium which the participants are using. Smileys evolved as a way of avoiding the ambiguities and misperceptions which come when written language is made to carry the burden of speech. They are brave efforts, but on the whole Netspeak lacks any true ability to signal facial meaning, and this, along with the unavailability of tones of voice, places it at a considerable remove from spoken language. One day, developments in interactive technology will allow us to see and hear other participants while they are talking, so that some of these limitations will be eliminated; but there will always be properties of the electronic medium which will enable us to use language in ways that traditional speech could never perform.

Not like writing

If Netspeak does not display the properties we would expect of speech, does it instead display the properties we expect of writing? Here too, there are fundamental differences. Let us consider first the space-bound character of traditional writing – the fact that a piece of text is static and permanent on the page. If something is written down, repeated reference to it will be an encounter with an unchanged text. We would be amazed if, upon returning to a particular page, it had altered its graphic character in some way. Putting it like this, we can see immediately that computer-mediated communication is not by any means like conventional writing. A 'page' on the Web often varies from encounter to encounter (and all have the option of varying, even if page-owners choose not to take it) for several possible reasons: its factual content might have been updated, its advertising sponsor might have changed, or its graphic designer might have added new features. Nor is the writing that you see necessarily static, given the technical options available which allow text to move around the screen, disappear/reappear, change colour, and so on. And from a user point of view, there are opportunities to 'interfere' with the text in all kinds of ways that are not possible in traditional writing. A page, once downloaded to the user's screen, may have its text cut, added to, revised, annotated, even totally restructured, in ways that make the result seem to come from the same source as the original. The possibilities are causing not a little anxiety among those concerned about issues of ownership, copyright and forgery.

The other Internet situations also display differences from traditional writing, with respect to their space-bound presence. E-mails are in principle static and permanent, but routine textual deletion is expected procedure (it is a prominent option in the management system), and it is possible to alter messages electronically with an ease and undetectability which is not possible when people try to alter a traditionally written text. What is especially revolutionary about e-mails is the way the medium permits what is called *framing*. We receive a message from M which contains, say, three different points in a single paragraph. We can, if we want, reply to each of these points by taking the paragraph, splitting it up into three parts, and then responding to each part separately, so that the message we send back to M then looks a bit like a play dialogue. Then, M can do the same thing to our responses, and when we get the message back, we see M's replies to what we sent. We can then send the lot on to someone else for further comments, and when it comes back, there are now three voices framed on the screen. And so it can go on – replies within replies within replies – and all unified within the same screen typography. There has never been anything like this in the history of human written communication. Although in principle it might have been possible to receive a letter, cut it up into strips, intercalate our responses, then paste everything onto another sheet of paper before returning it to its sender, this would hardly count as normal behaviour. But we do this all the time with e-mails, without thinking twice (once we are used to it).

Other features of computer-mediated communication take us even further away from traditional writing. Probably the most important is the *hypertext* link – the jump that users can make if they want to move from one page or site to another. The hypertext link is the most fundamental functional property of the Web, without which the medium would not exist. It does have parallels in some of the conventions of traditional written text. The use of note indicators is a sort of primitive hypertext link, moving the eye from one part of a page to another, or from one page of a text to another (if the notes are collected at the back of a book, as in the present volume, for example). The use within a sentence of bibliographical citations or cross-references (such as 'see p. 333') is another opportunity for a reader to break away from the conventions of linear viewing. But these features are marginal to traditional written language; we can easily think of texts which have no notes or cross-reference citations at all. The Web, by contrast, could not exist without its hypertext links. As Tim Berners-Lee once put it: 'Free speech in hypertext implies the "right to link", which is the very basic building unit for the whole Web.'[6] There is nothing in traditional written language which remotely resembles the dynamic flexibility and centrality of Web hypertext linkage.

A few other characteristics of traditional written language also display an uncertain relationship to Netspeak, but these hardly fall into the category of 'revolutionary'.

E-mails and chatgroup interactions, where the pressure is strong to communicate rapidly, lack the carefully planned, elaborate construction which is characteristic of so much writing. At one extreme, it might well appear that a revolution is taking place. Some people are happy to send messages with no revision at all, not caring if typing errors, erratic capitalization, lack of punctuation and other anomalies are included. This is actually a rather minor effect, which rarely interferes with intelligibility. It is patently a special style arising out of the pressures operating on users of the medium, plus a natural desire (especially among younger – or younger-minded – users) to be idiosyncratic and daring. And that is how it is perceived. If I receive an e-mail from M in which he mis-spells a word, I do not conclude from this that 'M can't spell'. I simply conclude that M is not a good typist or was in a hurry. I know this because I do the same thing myself when I am in a hurry. There is nothing truly revolutionary here. And it is, in any case, not a universal behaviour. There are many e-mailers who take as many pains to revise their messages as they would in non-Internet settings.

On the whole, Netspeak is better seen as written language which has been pulled some way in the direction of speech than as spoken language which has been written down. However, expressing the question in terms of the traditional dichotomy is itself misleading. Computer-mediated communication is not identical to either speech or writing, but selectively and adaptively displays properties of both. It also does things which neither of the other mediums does, presenting us with novel problems of information management. Consider, as an example, the *persistence* of a conversational message in a chatroom – the fact that it stays on the screen for a period of time (before the arrival of other messages replace it or make it scroll out of sight).

This certainly introduces novel properties to the inter-action which are not available in speech. It means, for example, that someone who enters a conversation a couple of turns after an utterance has been made can still see the utterance, reflect upon it, and react to it; the persistence is relatively short-lived, however, compared with that rou-tinely encountered in traditional writing. It also means, for those systems that provide an archiving log of all messages, in the order in which they were received by the server, that it is possible in principle to browse a past conversation, or search for a particular topic, in ways that spontaneous (unrecorded) conversation or traditional book-indexing does not permit.

Netspeak is more than an aggregate of spoken and written features. Because it does things that neither of these other mediums does, it has to be seen as a new species of communi-cation. It is more than just a hybrid of speech and writing, or the result of contact between two long-standing mediums. Electronic texts, of whatever kind, are simply not the same as other kinds of texts. They display fluidity, simultaneity (being available on an indefinite number of machines) and non-degradability in copying; they transcend the traditional limitations on textual dissemination; and they have perme-able boundaries (because of the way one text may be inte-grated within others or display links to others). Several of these properties have consequences for language, and these combine with those associated with speech and writing to make Netspeak a genuine 'new medium'.

The consequences of a new medium: within a language

The linguistic effects of the arrival of a new medium of communication are twofold: it initiates change in the formal character of the languages which use it; and it offers new opportunities for languages to use it. Of the two, it is the first which has attracted all the publicity with respect to the kind of language encountered on the Internet and in related technology, such as mobile phones (cellphones). The apparent lack of respect for the traditional rules of the written language has horrified some observers, who see in the development an ominous sign of deterioration in standards. Text-messaging is often cited as a particular problem. Children of the future will no longer be able to spell, it is said. However, the fact that youngsters abbreviate words in text-messaging using rebus techniques (*b4*, *CUl8er*), initialisms (*afaik* 'as far as I know', *imho* 'in my humble opinion') or respelling (*thx* 'thanks') is hardly new or fundamental. People have been using initialisms for generations (*ttfn*, *asap*, *fyi*), and rebus games have long been found in word-puzzle books. Even the fullest lists of text-message abbreviations contain no more than a few hundred forms, and few of those are commonly used. And because they were devised to meet the needs of economical messaging on a screen which has a limit of 160 characters, there is little motivation to use these deviant forms elsewhere. They lose their 'cool', group-identifying function when they are taken away from the technology, whether mobile phone or computer. The fact that a few kids might start using their abbreviations in places where they have no purpose – such as school essays – is something to be watched, of course. But that is what teaching needs to do. It has long been a principle of modern language teaching – whether foreign or mother-tongue – to inculcate in children a sense of linguistic responsibility and appropriateness. And children need to be taught, if they have failed to develop the intuition for themselves, that text-messaging abbreviations perform a useful function where space is tight and speed is critical, but not elsewhere.

The same point applies to the variations in the writing system that adults as well as children introduce into their e-mails. Many people use a severely reduced system, with virtually no typographic contrastivity at all. There are three main features. The status of *capitalization* varies greatly. Because most of the Internet is not case-sensitive, a random use of capitals has developed, or the use of no capitals at all. There is a strong tendency to use lower-case everywhere. The 'save a keystroke' principle is widely found in e-mails, chatgroups and virtual worlds, where whole sentences can be produced without capital letters marking the beginning of the sentence or proper names. *Punctuation* also tends to be minimalist, and is completely absent in some e-mails and chat exchanges. Here too, a lot depends on personality: some e-mailers are scrupulous about maintaining traditional punctuation; others use it when they have to, to avoid ambiguity; and some do not use it at all, either as a consequence of typing speed, or through not realizing that ambiguity can be one of the consequences. And *spelling* practice is also distinctive. In English, US spelling is more common than British, partly for historical reasons (the origins of the Internet), and partly for reasons of economy, most US spellings being a character shorter than British ones (*color* vs *colour*, *fetus* vs *foetus*, etc.). Nonstandard spelling, heavily penalized in traditional writing (at least, since the eighteenth century), is used without sanction in conversational settings. As already suggested, spelling errors in an e-mail would be assumed to be not an indication of lack of education (though they may be) but a function of typing inaccuracy.

I interpret these developments as extending the expressive range of the languages that are now on-line. Novel conventions are being introduced. This has always happened when a revolutionary communication technology has arrived. When printing was introduced, a whole range of new manifestations of written language emerged, including innovative layout conventions and punctuation usages, and a gradual standardization of spelling. When telephones arrived, new conventions of discourse inter-action had to be devised (saying hello, specifying or con-firming the number, etc.). When broadcasting arrived, spoken language diversified immensely, with results which today range from weather-forecasting style to sports commentary. And so it is now with the Internet, where the technology from the outset motivated new kinds of expres-sion. For example, the lower-case default mentality means that any use of capitalization is a strongly marked form of communication. Messages wholly in capitals are con-sidered to be 'shouting', and usually avoided; words in capitals add extra emphasis (with asterisks and spacing also available):

This is a VERY important point.
This is a * very * important point.
This is a v e r y important point.

Another distinctive feature of Internet graphology is the way two capitals are used – one initial, one medial – a phenomenon sometimes called *bicapitalization* (*BiCaps*), seen in such names as *AltaVista, PeaceNet* and *Compu-Serve*, or, more complexly, with *QuarkXPress*. There is an increased use of symbols not normally part of the trad-itional punctuation system, such as the #. Unusual com-binations of punctuation marks can occur, such as (to express pause) ellipsis dots (. . .) in any number, repeated hyphens (---) or the repeated use of commas (,,,,). Em-phasis and attitude can result in exaggerated or random use of punctuation, such as *!!!!!!!* or *£$£$%!*.

New vocabulary has also come into languages which are on-line, much of it deriving from the global use of English.

A large number of words and phrases have emerged which are needed to talk about Internet-restricted situations, operations, activities and personnel, making this one of the most creative lexical domains in contemporary English, and analogous developments are taking place in other languages, as they increase their on-line presence. Many terms are associated with the software which enables people to use the Internet, and which routinely appear on screen. Some have a permanent presence (albeit in hidden menus), in the form of the labels used to designate screen areas and functions, and to specify user options and commands: *file, edit, view, insert, paste, format, tools, window, help, search, refresh, address, history, stop, contact, top, back, forward, home, send, save, open, close, select, toolbars, fonts, options.* Some terms appear only at intervals on a screen, depending on circumstances – usually, when things are going wrong, in the form of error messages (there seem to be no positive messages to tell us that everything is going right): *forbidden, illegal operation, error, not found, 404 error* ['a page or site is no longer in service']. Several terms are associated with the use of computer hardware: *freeze, lock, down, hang, crash, bomb, client* (the machine, not the user). And terms have emerged for the population of Internet users themselves: *netizens, netters, netties, netheads, cybersurfers, nerds, newbies, surfers, digiterati.* Many of these words are everyday terms which have been given a fresh sense in an Internet context.

A popular method of creating Internet neologisms is to combine two separate words to make a new word, or *compound.* Some elements turn up repeatedly – for example, *click* in *click-and-buy, one-click, cost-per-click, double-click, clickthrough rate,* and so on. Similar in function are the use of *cyber-* and *hyper-* in such words as *cyberspace, cyberculture, cyberlawyer, cybersex, cybersquatter, cyberian, cyber rights; hypertext, hyperlink, hyperfiction* and *hyperzine.*

Blends (in which part of one word is joined to part of another) are illustrated by *netiquette, infonet, datagram, infobahn* and *Internaut*. An innovation is the retaining of the period found in electronic addresses within certain compounds, as a kind of infix, seen in *net.legend, net.abuse* and *net.citizen*, or sites beginning with *alt*. (with the punctuation mark often spoken aloud as 'dot'). Acronyms are very common: a tiny sample would include *BBS* ['bulletin board system'], *BCC* ['blind carbon copy'], *DNS* ['domain name system'], *FAQ* ['frequently asked questions'], *HTML* ['hypertext markup language'], *ISP* ['Internet Service Provider'], *URL* ['uniform resource locator'], and the names of many firms and sites, such as *AOL, IBM* and *IRC*. Letter-plus-number combinations are also found: *W3C* ['World Wide Web Consortium'], *P3P* ['Platform for Privacy Preferences'] and *Go2Net*.

It is always a sure sign that a new variety has 'arrived' when people in other linguistic situations start alluding to it in speech. It is therefore of considerable interest to note the way in which features of Netspeak have already begun to be used outside of the situation of computer-mediated communication, even though the medium has become available to most people only in the past decade or so. In everyday conversation, terms from the underlying computer technology are given a new application among people who want their talk to have a cool cutting-edge. Examples from recent overheard conversations include *It's my turn to download now* ('I've heard all your gossip, now hear mine'), *I need more bandwidth to handle that point* ('I can't take it all in at once'), *Get with the programme* ('Keep up') and *She's multi-tasking* ('She's doing several things at once'). Resonances are now routine on radio and television: presenters commonly add e-addresses when telling listeners and viewers how they might contact a programme, using *at*, *dot* and *forward slash* to punctuate their utterance. *Dot com* is now a commonly heard phrase, as well as appearing ubiquitously in writing in all kinds of advertising and promotional material. And the *e-* prefix is now encountered in thousands of expressions, such as *e-text*, *e-zine*, *e-cash*, *e-government*, *e-bandwagon*, *e-books*, *e-conferences* and *e-voting*. In 1998 the American Dialect Society named *e-* 'Word [*sic*] of the Year' as well as 'Most Useful and Most Likely to Succeed'.

How many of these developments will become a permanent feature of English in the twenty-first century it is impossible to say. The same point applies to the impact of the Internet on other languages. We can never predict language change, only recognize it once it has happened. But it is already evident that, since the 1990s, a notion of Netspeak has begun to evolve which is rapidly becoming a part of popular linguistic consciousness, and evoking strong language attitudes. This is bound to grow as the century proceeds.

The consequences of a new medium: for all languages

There is a further reason for the revolutionary status of the Internet – the fact that it offers a home to *all* languages – as soon as their communities have a functioning computer technology, of course. Its increasingly multilingual character has been the most notable change since it started out, not very long ago, as a totally English medium. There is a story that the 8-year-old son of Kyrgyzstan's President Akayev told his father that he had to learn English. When asked why, the child apparently replied: 'Because, daddy, the computer speaks English.'

For many, indeed, the language of the Internet *is* English. There was a headline in *The New York Times* in 1996 which said simply: 'World, Wide, Web: 3 English Words'. The article went on to say: 'if you want to take full advantage of the Internet there is only one real way to do it: learn English.'[7] This view is no longer valid. With the Internet's globalization, the presence of other languages has steadily risen. By 1998, a widely quoted figure was that about 80 per cent of the Net was in English. This figure derived from the first major study of language distribution on the Internet, carried out in the previous year by Babel, a joint initiative of the Internet Society and Alis Technologies. This showed English well ahead, but with several other languages entering the ring – notably German, Japanese, French and Spanish. Since then, the estimates for English have been steadily falling. A recent Global Reach survey estimated that people with Internet access in non-English-speaking countries increased between 1995 and 2000 from 7 million to 136 million. In 1998, there was another surprise: the number of newly created Web sites *not* in English passed the total for newly created sites that *were* in English. And at a conference on Search Engine Strategies in London in 2000, a representative of AltaVista was predicting that by the end of 2002 less than 50 per cent of the Web would be in English. This has turned out to be the case. In certain parts of the world, the local language is already dominant. According to one Japanese Internet author, Yoshi Mikami, 90 per cent of Web pages in Japan are already in Japanese.

It is not surprising to see the Web (and the Internet as a whole) becoming predominantly *non*-English as communications infrastructure develops in Asia, Africa and South America. This is where the bulk of the people are. The Web is increasingly reflecting the distribution of language presence in the real world, and many sites provide the evidence. There are thousands of businesses now doing their best to present a multilingual identity, and hundreds of major sites collecting all kinds of data on the languages themselves. Call up the font archive at the University of Oregon, for example: you'll find 112 printing fonts in their archives for over forty languages. They have a nice sense of humour too – because you'll also find some data there on alien languages, such as Klingon, and folklore languages, such as Elvish, which Tolkien invented for *The Lord of the Rings*. Spend an hour hunting for languages on the World Wide Web and you will find hundreds. In 2001 I spent a few days tracking down as many examples as I could find, for my book *Language and the Internet*. I found one site, called World Language Resources, which listed products for 728 languages. I found an African resource list which covered several local languages: Yoruba, for example, was illustrated by some 5,000 words, along with proverbs, naming patterns and greetings. Another site dealt with no less than eighty-seven European minority languages. Some of the sites were very small in content, of course, but nonetheless extensive in range: one gave the Lord's Prayer in nearly 500 languages.

Nobody has yet worked out just how many languages have obtained a modicum of presence on the Web. I found over 1,000 quite quickly. It is not difficult to find evidence of an Internet presence for all the more frequently used languages in the world, and for a large number of minority languages too. My guess is that at least a quarter of the world's languages – about 1,500 – have some sort of cyber-existence now. And this is language presence in a real sense. These are not sites which only analyse or talk about languages, from the point of view of linguistics or some other academic subject. They are sites which allow us to see languages as they are. In many cases, the total Web presence, in terms of number of pages, is quite small.

The crucial point is that the languages *are* out there, even if they are represented by only a sprinkling of sites.

The Internet is the ideal medium for minority languages, and this is a lifeline which could prove to be important for some of the languages whose plight was described in chapter 2. If you are a speaker or supporter of an endangered language – an aboriginal language, say, or one of the Celtic languages – you are keen to give the language some publicity, to draw its plight to the attention of the world. Previously, this was very difficult to do. It was hard to attract a newspaper article on the subject, and the cost of a newspaper advertisement was prohibitive. It was virtually impossible to get a radio or television programme devoted to it. But now, with Web pages and e-mail waiting to be used, you can get your message out in next to no time, in your own language – with a translation as well, if you want – and in front of a global audience whose potential size makes traditional media audiences look minuscule by comparison. The Web message stays around, too, in a way that newspaper and broadcasting references do not. Chat rooms, moreover, are a boon to speakers living in isolation from each other, as now there can be a virtual speech community to which they can belong. Several of the world's 'smaller' languages that have access to Internet technology – such as the minority languages of Europe and many North American Indian languages – now have Web sites and foster virtual speech communities.

On the other hand, I have to recognize that developing a significant cyber-presence for a language is not easy. To begin with, the infrastructure has to be there – and with so many endangered languages existing in parts of the world where the electricity supply is unreliable or non-existent, the priorities are clear. Then, to use present-day Web technology, the language has to be written down, and as we have seen in chapter 2, this excludes some 2,000

languages which have not been documented at all. Another complication is that the distinctive letters of some
languages (especially those which make use of a range of
accent marks) are often not easily encodable so that they
can be routinely 'read' by computers everywhere. Lastly,
even if there is the technology and the literacy, there is a
hurdle of motivation to be crossed. There seems to be
a sort of 'critical mass' of Internet penetration which has
to build up in a country or community before a language
develops a vibrant cyber-life. It is not much use, really, to
have just one or two sites in a local language on the Web.
People wanting to use or find out about the language
would soon get bored. The number of sites has to build
up until, suddenly, everybody is using them and adding to
them and talking about them. That is a magic moment,
and only a few hundred languages have so far reached it.
In the jargon of the Internet, there needs to be lots of good
'content' in the local languages out there, and until there
is, people will stay using the languages that have managed
to accumulate content – English, in particular.

So the character of a multilingual Internet is still evolving, and likely to be one of the main points of development
in the next few years. Everything depends on how quickly
new sites can build up a local language momentum. And
we must not underestimate the practical difficulties. Take,
for example, the apparently simple issue of representing a
language's letters accurately. Until quite recently there
were real problems in using the characters of the keyboard
to cope with the alphabetical diversity of the world's languages. Because it was the English alphabet that was the
standard, only a very few non-English symbols could be
handled. If it was a foreign word with some strange-
looking accent marks, the Internet software would simply
ignore them, and assume they weren't important. This can
still happen – but there have been important develop-

ments. First, the basic set of keyboard characters, the so-called ASCII set, was extended, so that the commoner non-English accents could be included. Even then it only allowed up to 256 characters – and there are far more letter or word shapes in the world than that. Just think of the array of shapes you find in Arabic, Hindi, Chinese, Korean and the many other languages which do not use the Roman alphabet. Today, a new coding, the UNICODE system, is much more sophisticated: in its latest version it allows the representation on screen of over 94,000 characters – though that is still well short of the total number of written characters in all the world's languages, which has been estimated to be about 175,000.

My feeling is that the future looks good for Web multilingualism, and this opinion seems to be becoming widespread. Ned Thomas, for instance, is editor of a bulletin called *Contact* – the quarterly publication of the European Bureau of Lesser Used Languages. In an editorial in 2000 he said: 'It is not the case . . . that all languages will be marginalized on the Net by English. On the contrary, there will be a great demand for multilingual Web sites, for multilingual data retrieval, for machine translation, for voice recognition systems to be multilingual.'[8] And Tyler Chambers, the creator of various Web language projects, agrees: 'the future of the Internet', he says, 'is even more multilingualism and cross-cultural exploration and understanding than we've already seen.'[9] I concur. The Web offers a World Wide Welcome for global linguistic diversity. And in an era when so many languages of the world are dying, such optimism is truly revolutionary.

4

After the Revolution

The three trends described in earlier chapters – the emergence of a global language, the phenomenon of language endangerment and the arrival of the Internet – have had consequences for our developing notions of linguistic diversity. Global English has given extra purpose to a variety of Standard English in the way it guarantees a medium of international intelligibility; but it has also fostered the growth of local varieties as a means of expressing regional identity, and some of these new varieties will, in due course, evolve into new languages. The Internet has provided us with a new linguistic medium which provides a completely fresh range of expressive possibilities, as well as offering novel dimensions of stylistic variation and new ways of focusing on language use. There is even an up-side to language endangerment: the manifestation of language death on such a scale has sharpened the minds of minority language users wonderfully, and fresh initiatives are now everywhere – not least the one which led to the European Year of Languages – to influence public opinion about what linguistic identity means and how it can be fostered. The potential is present for great things to happen. But, as always with revolutions, it is up to individuals to capitalize on them. And to do this we have to rethink several of our long-established notions about the nature of language. It is not always a comfortable process.

The most important rethinking arises out of what happens if we take the axiom of the European Year of Languages seriously and really think it through. I take this axiom to be the recognition that multilingualism (often referred to as plurilingualism) in general, and bilingualism in particular, is an intrinsic good. I relate this axiom to the postulate that multilingualism is the normal human condition. Depending on what we mean by bilingualism, which I discuss below, estimates for the number of people in the world who are bilingual range from 50 per cent (for a high-level competence) to 80 per cent (for some level of competence). A significant number use three or more languages. This seems to be prima facie evidence for the view that children are born not just with a LAD (= Language Acquisition Device), as Chomsky argued, but with a MAD (= Multilingual Acquisition Device), the acronym avoiding the ambiguity that it is just one language that children are ready to acquire. Rather, the reality seems to be that there is no limit to the number of languages that a child will pick up once exposed to them. From the young child's point of view, of course, the fact that they are different languages is immaterial. They are simply different ways of speaking. We adults know they are different languages, but it is not until children are in the fourth year of life that they become aware of this and start to manipulate the different languages to personal advantage.

Thinking through the notion of multilingualism means, first of all, recognizing that it is not homogeneous. Learning a language is a multi-tasking experience, involving in its fullest form four modes – listening, speaking, reading and writing (deaf signing, of course, is a fifth mode in certain circumstances). It is perfectly possible to develop a multilingual competence in only the first two of these modes – indeed, in some 40 per cent of the world's languages, as we have seen, the users have no choice, because their languages have never been written down. It is also possible to develop just a 'reading' knowledge of a language. And differentials between the active and passive modes within spoken and written language are also common: people who listen better than they speak, and who read better than they write. The notion of multilingualism cannot be restricted to people who are fluent in all four modes, as this would exclude a significant proportion of the world's population whose lives actually function through the use of more than one language. Rather, multilingualism has to allow for ability in any subset of the modes.

It also has to allow for varying levels of ability within a mode. Learning a language involves minimally the learning of pronunciation, grammar and vocabulary (to restrict the point to just these three traditional domains). Let us call the total acquisition of each of these domains '100 per cent fluency' – that is, a speaker can pronounce all the sounds, use all the grammatical constructions, and know all the vocabulary available in a (dialect of a) language. On that basis, of course, no-one is totally fluent, for no-one knows the million or so words in English, for example; and even some of its 3,500 or so grammatical constructions will not be comfortably used by everyone (e.g. some of the more complex instructions of literary or legal English), nor will some of the more sophisticated tone-of-voice effects (e.g. those used by actors). Plainly we make all kinds of allowances in talking about fluency, and operate with a notional scale from 0 to 100 per cent within each of these areas. We then (also notionally) synthesize a combined total for the language as a whole, so that we are prepared to rate Ms X as being 'more fluent' than Mr Y. But there is no way of evaluating whether Mr A, who is strong in grammar and weak in vocabulary, is 'more' or 'less' fluent than Ms B, who is weak in grammar and strong in vocabulary. The number of possibilities is immense. Both Mr A and Ms B are bilingual, to an extent – and are certainly 'more bilingual' than Mr C, who has no ability in any area. Only this relativistic conception of bilingualism makes sense of what we actually see in the world.

And what we see, when we look around, is a world where different levels of linguistic demand are made on people. A commonplace notion, for example, includes 'survival ability' in a language, or a notion of 'getting by'. People use these notions all the time, assessing their strengths as greater or weaker in certain areas and languages. We all know how difficult it is to answer the question, 'How many languages do you speak?' or '... do you know?' We all want to hedge straight away. This is to recognize the reality of bilingualism, that it is not an all-or-none phenomenon, but a dynamic mixture of different levels of ability, constantly changing as we change our circumstances, gain or lose our opportunities to use a language, or, quite simply, grow old. When we hear everyone hedging in this way if asked apparently straightforward questions such as 'Do you speak X?' or 'Are you bilingual?', then we must be asking the wrong questions. Any theory of bilingualism that wants to be taken seriously has to recognize this indeterminacy.

The recognition of indeterminacy brings into centre-stage a notion that has been much neglected, but whose significance is bound to grow in the twenty-first century – semilingualism. The term has been used in several ways. It can mean people who have not achieved high levels of native fluency in *any* language – one is reminded of Salvatore, in Umberto Eco's *The Name of the Rose*, who spoke 'all languages and no language' – usually because they have been extremely mobile as children, and never lived long enough in a place to have a stable family or community background. Thousands of migrant families, travellers, asylum seekers and refugees fall into this category. They must not be excluded from our notion of multilingualism just because their linguistic world is different. More common are those people who live their lives in a multilingual community but who for some reason are unable (or unwilling) to achieve high levels of achievement in all the languages of that community. A common situation is a youngster who learns a second language (L2) at home or in primary school, then leaves home to find work in an area where L2 is not used, and returns in later life with a semilingual command of L2. This is a form of bilingualism too. A third situation is illustrated by the typical scenario in Africa, where a community may make routine use of several languages, but the use of each is related to a particular social situation. One language might be used at home, another in the market-place, a third in church, a fourth in school, and so on. However, the point is that the 'amount' of language someone might need to 'survive' or 'perform' in any one of these contexts might be very different from the corresponding amount needed in the others. Indeed it may be very little – as in the days when a very restricted range of Latin expressions was actively used in the Roman Catholic Church. But someone who competently uses a language in a restricted way cannot be excluded from our multilingualism tally. Quite considerable levels of language ability may be present – but still a long way from what we would count as 100 per cent fluency. Such limited levels would not have much survival value in a context like the European Union, for example, where there is a demand for total translation equivalence. But the European situation is a rather special case.

This demand for total translation equivalence – the principle that everything which can be said in one language should be available in another – also needs some rethinking. It is common for someone to have an experience in one language which they are unable to talk about in another, because they do not know the relevant vocabulary or idiom (as already noted in chapter 1, with the example of the French-speaking mother in England). In the African case above, people who routinely experience the marketplace context might have a strongly developed vegetable vocabulary, for example, which they lack in the language that they encounter in church. It simply would not be possible for the people to carry on a sophisticated conversation in their church language about cabbages – nor, one imagines, would they ever need to. Only in certain circumstances – where there are certain legal constraints, for example, or where people are worried about competition between languages in a public arena – does the demand for total translational equivalence make sense. The idea of 'translating everything' is an unusual one. Multilingualism has not evolved to enable us to translate everything into everything else. It has evolved to meet the pragmatic communicative needs of individual people and communities. Sometimes translation is useful; sometimes it is unnecessary; sometimes it is positively undesirable; and sometimes it is absolutely impracticable.

It is the last criterion, of course, which produces the dilemma faced by the European Union as its membership grows into the mid-twenties. There is no solution to such dilemmas if our mindset is conditioned by a 'translate everything' paradigm. Solutions can be found only if this paradigm is replaced by one which recognizes some sort of pragmatically guided selectivity in the context of a lingua franca. A pragmatic paradigm asserts that we translate when it is useful to do so, and not because 'everything must be translated'. The various criteria for defining 'useful' need to be thought about, of course. Some items (documents, speeches) will be crucial because they relate to a country's perception of its identity. Some will be crucial because they encapsulate legal content which needs to be present in every language. Some will be useful only to certain countries (e.g. a document about coastal defences is presumably of limited interest to countries which have no coastline). It is an axiom that every country has the status of its language respected. But it does not follow from this that everything has to be translated. As a theoretical case: if there are twenty documents, and four language communities (who share a lingua franca, of course), and documents 1–5 are translated into L1, documents 6–10 into L2, and so on, then everyone is being treated equally, and respect is shared, though none have all documents translated. How far such a model can be implemented in practice, given political sensitivities, is unclear; but it is plain that respect, like translation, is a pragmatic notion.

This kind of reasoning scares people, because the brave new world it points towards is unfamiliar and untested. But it is the nature of revolutions to present people with the need for new paradigms. And currently we are experiencing a linguistic revolution in which old models are being replaced by new ones, and a transitional period which is inevitably one of great uncertainty. People are unclear about the role of a truly global lingua franca, because they have never experienced one before. They are seeing the loss of languages around the world, and are not sure what to do. And they are faced with new and unexplored technologies which they have limited experience in handling. Teachers, at the cutting-edge of language work, routinely bemoan their plight. A typical remark: 'In the old days there was American English and British English, and I knew where I was; now, I've no idea where I am.' But everyone, not just teachers, is faced with the uncertainties of a rapidly changing linguistic world. As a result there is an understandable tendency to dig the heels in, to take up extreme positions, and to make traditional notions (such as the notion of a language having 'official status') bear a weight which they were never designed to carry. The result is what we see: huge quantities of unread translations; vast amounts of time wasted and points left unsaid because people feel the need to say everything twice in a speech (once in their own language and again in the lingua franca); and the covert use of 'relay languages' and 'working languages' to make sure jobs get done (which insidiously eats away at the principle of respecting linguistic diversity). Far better, it seems to me, is for people to work towards replacing absolutist conceptions by relativistic ones – the concept of 'official language', for example, being replaced by 'official for a particular purpose', and to spend the time trying to work out what these purposes might be.

These directions of thinking are uncomfortable, also, because it is the nature of linguistic reality to be uncomfortable, especially in a revolutionary era, where change is so rapid and universal. Relativistic notions bear little resemblance to the black-and-white world that linguistic purists inhabit. And the world of multilingualism is full of purists – people who believe that there exists some form of a language which is intrinsically superior to all others and which it is their duty to protect against change, especially against the influence of other languages (and most especially against English). There is an element of the purist in all of us, but it is an element which we have to control, for the historical reality is clear: that all languages change, that all borrow from each other, and that there is no such thing as a 'pure' language, and never has been. English, indeed, is the borrower par excellence, as it were, as we have seen in chapter 1. But borrowing is often viewed as anathema by puristically minded supporters of a language, because they feel that their language is somehow debased if it uses words from other languages. Purists have a very short community memory: they forget that, a generation before, several forms of the language that they now accept as standard were contentious.

As we saw in chapter 2, the point is especially sensitive between old and young generations, the former insisting on 'correctness' and the latter wishing to make use of 'cool' loan words (often from English). In a 'healthy' language, with millions of speakers, purist attitudes cause no harm, because they are swallowed up in the myriad opinions which comprise the speech community. Indeed, they probably have an important role to play, identifying one pole of a spectrum of opinion which allows other positions to be more clearly seen by contrast. There is a 'descriptive' position in linguistics, for instance, which asserts that all usage – whether standard or nonstandard – is valid. This position becomes more sharply defined when it is seen in contradistinction to the 'prescriptive' view, which asserts that only certain usages – those sanctioned by respected grammars and dictionaries – are valid. But when we are dealing with minority and endangered languages, purism becomes harmful. My view is unequivocal: any speech community which allows the purist mentality to dominate its linguistic policy is signing the death warrant for its language. The teenagers are the parents of the next generation of children, and if the language is to be passed on, these are the ones who have to be persuaded that there is a point. But each time 'their' language is rejected by community elders because it is 'incorrect', this vitality is reduced. It is another nail in the coffin.

It has to be accepted that the identity of a language will change – as it always has in the past – even, as we saw in chapter 2, to the extent of fundamentally altering its char-

acter. This apparently unpalatable truth can be made less
so by pointing to what happens when languages actually
do change their character. They do not somehow deterior-
ate or disappear; rather, their new character becomes a
fresh resource which can be used in all kinds of creative
directions. English, as we have seen, provides the classic
case. The result of adding huge amounts of Classical and
Romance vocabulary to English has not been the deterioration of English; on the contrary, what we now have is a
lexicon with a hugely increased range of expressiveness,
enabling fresh opportunities for creativity. Ironically, it is
the Classical lexicon which many people (though not
George Orwell) feel adds 'quality' to English. The language of the next generation is never the same as the
language of its predecessor. And accepting the inevitabil-
ity, if not desirability, of change is an essential part of any
realistic approach to multilingualism. Part of the new
mindset of a post-revolutionary era has, accordingly, to
be the acceptance of much greater levels of contact effects
(such as loan words), and a preparedness to encounter
huge numbers of 'code-mixed' languages in which massive
intermixing has taken place (as in Singlish's use of English
and Chinese).

Casting the argument in terms of an opposition between
'old' and 'young', or 'correct' and 'cool', is itself a distor-
tion. The two positions are not totally exclusive. It is
perfectly possible to have a linguistic situation in which a
highly colloquial and 'cool' level of language use exists
alongside a highly formal and 'correct' level. This kind of
situation is captured by the notion of tri-dialectism described at the end of chapter 1, and also by the notion of
two very different versions of a language existing at the
same time (*diglossia*), illustrated by such cases as Classical
vs Colloquial Arabic or Swiss vs High German. It is likely
that languages will become increasingly diglossic (even

triglossic, with three simultaneously existing versions) as contact effects increase, and these will be particularly noticeable in minority languages, where the smaller number of speakers will make the different levels stand out more prominently. Only an inclusive language policy can cope with such developments. Any policy which operates exclusively – declaring that a certain group of speakers does not speak the 'proper' language – is on a course of self-destruction. A minority language needs every friend it can get, regardless of the kind or level of language the speakers display. Someone who has just put their foot on the bilingual ladder (with 1 per cent fluency, in the above terms) is to be welcomed and valued. Unfortunately, the surprising truth is that historical conceptions of ownership can get in the way of inclusiveness. 'They have no right to learn our language' is an attitude often heard by traditionalists faced with incomers. The position is complex, and not entirely without point, but it is ultimately self-defeating.

The more we explore the notion of multilingualism in a post-revolutionary linguistic world, the more we find our cherished notions having to be revised or even jettisoned. Even such fundamental notions as the distinction between 'native' and 'non-native' languages, or between 'first', 'second' and 'foreign' languages, have to be rethought. The situation referred to in chapter 1 provides an example: babies are now being born all over the world who are being taught language by parents of mixed-language backgrounds, for whom English is an essential lingua franca. In other words the babies are going to be learning 'English as a foreign language' as a mother-tongue. Such developments can take even language professionals by surprise. What professionals need to appreciate is the even greater levels of rethinking which have to take place among the general public, where, for example, the notion that monolingualism is the norm is surprisingly pervasive (especially in those countries which have a recent history of colonialism). Among politicians and administrators there is a natural tendency to look for neat and simple solutions – devising formulae, for example, about how many languages it is desirable for a country to teach or work towards. But notions of 'L1 + 1' (learn one foreign language in addition to your own), 'L1 + 2', or whatever, bear little relationship to the real world, where people operate with as many languages as they need and at a variety of levels. To my mind, the only concept which relates well to the multilingual world I see around me is that of the *language portfolio* – a notion now quite widely used in Europe which focuses on the range of languages and competences which a person has available. It is this which needs to be operationalized in school curricula and elsewhere.

To cope with revolutions we need a strategy which is sufficiently flexible to integrate many levels and types of users. Its focus has to be on 'ordinary families' and on children at home, because this is where languages are most solidly acquired; but homes have to be seen in the context of communities (real or virtual) to avoid isolationism, and so local community initiatives need to play their part. It is this local focus which provides a means of integrating the different approaches that people use when they are engaged in language planning. In relation to chapter 2, I referred to the role of the arts as a significant strategy in focusing public attention on linguistic issues, especially in relation to endangered languages, and this point is taken up below. In chapter 3 I referred to the corresponding revitalizing potential of the electronic medium. But the home is the only place where all such factors are routinely present. The appreciation of art begins at home, from the simplest forms of home decor and body art to more advanced forms of music, pictures, story-telling and film. The appreciation of Internet technology is increasingly based in the home, and will significantly grow with the spread of broadband communication. So it is in the home and local community where the effects of the linguistic revolution are going to be most apparent.

The arts and language death

'Focusing public attention on linguistic issues, especially in relation to endangered languages.' How is this to be done? Anyone who works in the conservation field knows that the raising of public awareness is the most difficult goal to achieve. It has taken the ecological movement as a whole over a century to bring the world to its present state of consciousness about endangered plant and animal species. For example, the National Audubon Society in the US was founded in 1866: we have been bird-aware for nearly 150 years. For world heritage sites, we have the highly successful UNESCO programme, begun in 1972. Greenpeace, the year before, 1971. The World Wildlife Fund, 1961. The World Conservation Union, 1948. It took over thirty years before this Union was able to establish a World Conservation Strategy (1980), which led to the principles laid down in the 1991 document *Caring for the Earth*.

Compared with such time-frames, linguistic achievements by way of consciousness-raising within just a decade have been remarkable indeed. Thanks to an enormous amount of effort by a fairly small number of individuals and institutions, and the availability of new communication technology, we have made great progress in relation to the three criteria which we know must be present before progress can be made with an endangered language. First, there is what might be called the 'bottom-up' interest – the speech community itself must want its language saved – and there are now many recorded accounts of how attitudes can be sensitively managed and energies channelled to ensure that this happens. Second, there must be 'top-down' interest: the local and national government need to be in sympathy with the philosophy of language revitalization and supportive of the task in hand. 'Top-down' also includes obtaining the support of international political organizations, such as UNESCO and the Council of Europe, who are crucial in forming an appropriate political climate within which pressure can be brought to bear in difficult situations. We need only reflect for a moment on the number of political statements which were made during the 1990s, such as the 1996 Barcelona Declaration, to realize that enormous progress has been made in this respect – but we are still, it seems, some way from the goal of an unequivocal United Nations statement of human linguistic rights.

But neither bottom-up nor top-down support is enough without the third criterion – cash. We know that implementing a minority language policy is expensive, in the short term. In the long term, of course, any policy of balanced multilingualism, in which minority languages are respected and protected, guarantees massive savings – if for no other reason than by avoiding the huge expenditure (often in terms of life as well as money) which arises when people, seeing their linguistic identity threatened, take civil action to protect themselves and their future. But the initial outlay does cost money – not huge amounts, as we saw in chapter 2, but enough to put governments off, and enough to give support organizations (such as the Endangered Language Fund) a tough time finding capital to make even a small contribution to the present need. That is why the efforts of the large organizations, such as the Volkswagen Stiftung and the Lisbet Rausing Charitable Fund, which are donating significant sums to the documentation of endangered languages in the new millennium, have to be loudly applauded. But the question remains: why are there not more such organizations involved? Why, if language conservation is the intellectual equivalent of biological conservation, have we yet made so little progress in obtaining the requisite funding? The World Conservation Union had a budget of 140 million Swiss francs in 2002, and many millions more go into the support of biological conservation projects worldwide. Compared with that, the support for linguistic projects is so far minuscule. Why?

The answer, I believe, is that still very few people are aware of the existence and the scale of the problem. And there are large numbers of the general population who still need to be persuaded that the situation *is* a problem. The Babel myth referred to in chapter 2 – that a single language on earth guarantees a mutually intelligible and therefore peaceful planet – is still widely believed. And many of the people who are unaware of the language crisis are the opinion-formers of this world – journalists, politicians, media personalities, business leaders and others. I doubt whether there is anyone in the thinking world who is not now aware, even if only dimly, of the crisis facing the world's bio-ecology. By contrast, only a tiny proportion of these people have any awareness at all of the crisis in linguistic ecology. How many *do* know? In preparing a radio programme on the topic during the late 1990s, I asked a series of passers-by in the street whether they were aware that so many of the world's languages were dying. The people who claimed to be aware (whether they really were or not I do not know) were one in four. The other three had no idea what I was talking about. A similar exercise at the University of Manchester got the same result. Seventy-five per cent of the population seem not to know that there is an issue, therefore. And a fair number of the remaining twenty-five per cent do not believe that it is an important issue. How can the message best be communicated to them?

Lectures, books and radio programmes are the traditional ways – but these have limited effect. Even if one of the academic books on this topic sold out, we would be talking only about a few thousand copies. Books like my *Language Death* do not get into Christmas must-buy best-selling lists. Academic textbooks have an important role in forming intellectual opinion, but they are not the way of raising public awareness, and certainly not if we are in a hurry. We have to look in other directions. In fact there are several ways of achieving this goal, but the most important of them we have hardly begun to explore, and certainly not at an institutional level. I cite four as primary: using the media, the arts, the Internet and the school curriculum. All four need to be involved in any systematic effort to bring public awareness about linguistic ecology to the same level as that which exists in the biological domain.

Some progress has been made with reference to the first way: enlisting the support of the media. There has in fact been increased interest shown by some sections of the media as a result of the revolutionary decade. Several articles have appeared in general-interest magazines and newspapers. There have been pieces, often illustrated with stunning photographs, in such periodicals as *Civilization*, *Prospect*, *National Geographic*, *Scientific American*, and even the British Airways in-flight magazine, *High Life*. Radio has also served the topic well. From 2000–1 I know of a dozen or so radio programmes devoted to the topic of language death on the BBC's two main documentary channels, Radio 3 or Radio 4 – in one case a series (called *Lost for Words*) of four half-hour programmes. There seems to have been similar radio interest elsewhere: I am aware of programmes made in the United States, Canada and Australia, and there must be several more in other countries. Television, by contrast, has been less interested. Since the mid-1990s I know of ten proposals to the various UK television channels for documentaries or mini-series on language death, and although three of these reached a quite advanced stage of preparation – including in one case scripted and partly filmed material – none ever reached completion. The only success story was the component on language death which was included in the series *Beyond Babel*, produced by Infonation (the former film-making branch of the UK Foreign and Common-wealth Office), which was screened in over fifty countries in 2002, and which is now available on DVD. This was, ironically, an account of how English has become a world language; but the producers were sensible enough to accept the argument that there was another side of the coin.

The television failure is part of a broader scenario. There has never (as of 2003) been a television blockbuster series on the general topic of language, as such, anywhere in the world. There have of course been individual programmes on some of the 'sexier' aspects of language – such as child language acquisition, or sign language, or speech disability. And there have been a number of series or programmes on individual languages. English, as we might expect, gets the most attention. *The Story of English* appeared in the 1980s – a huge eight-hour transatlantic co-production – and another eight-hour epic, *The Adventure of English*, appeared on UK television in 2002–3, telling the same story in a very similar way. A few other individual languages have attracted interest too. A six-part series, *The Story of Welsh*, was shown on BBC Wales in 2003; and there have been similar programmes on Breton, Irish and a number of other European minority languages, as well as on the indigenous languages of Australia, the USA and Canada.

But in all these cases, the creative energy is entirely inward-looking. These programmes tell the story of endangerment only as it affects the individual communities – the Welsh, the Bretons or whoever. None of them takes the requisite step back and looks at the language endangerment situation as a whole. The nearest we get is when a programme deals with more than one language together, such as a programme made for the Netherlands TV network, in 2001, which looked at the similar plights of Welsh and Frisian, and inevitably began to generalize as a consequence. Another is an ongoing project by the Czech filmmaker Michael Havas, whose project on a single Brazilian language spoken by the Krenak tribe, 'Brazilian Dream', is conceived as a symbol of the world situation. Such perspectives are rare. It seems very difficult to get people who are desperately anxious about the state of their own language to devote some of their energy to considering the broader picture. It is short-sighted, because each endangered language can learn something from the situation of other languages – why some languages seem to be doing better than others. Nonetheless, in 2003 our theme still awaits effective television treatment.

Having had the opportunity to talk these issues over with several television companies, over the years, I have a sense of why there is such reluctance. There is a widely held view that language is too abstract and complex a subject for television treatment. On probing further, it usually transpires that the decision-makers are either thinking back to their days of studying grammar in school (much of broadcasting senior management is of the age when they had to parse sentences and study prescriptive grammar) or they have had a close encounter of the third kind with Chomsky, and it has scared them. They are also worried by the generality of the subject: that language does not fit neatly into a TV niche, such as current affairs, or comedy. They are petrified by the risk of the academic approach making people switch off. Even though there have been highly successful TV series by academics and other intellectuals – Michael Wood's series on Shakespeare, Simon Schama's on history, Lord Winston's on medicine and evolution – when it comes to language, the eyes glaze over. Even the specific-language programmes are affected. Language programmes are presented not by linguists but by personalities whose primary reputation lies elsewhere – *The Adventure of English* by the novelist and arts presenter Melvyn Bragg; *The Story of Welsh* by the newsreader Huw Edwards. If the early decades of the twenty-first century do eventually see a TV series on language death, heaven knows who they will get to present it – Oprah Winfrey, probably.

But would that be a bad thing? If the content is right and the quality is assured, then a big media personality would probably do the subject the world of good. Bottom-up, top-down, cash – the three criteria will all operate at their best if a profound awareness of the nature and likelihood of language death enters the general population, and personalities can help make this happen. But it is more than awareness that is wanted. We also need enthusiasm. People have to be enthused about the issues surrounding language death. Their emotions as well as their intellects have to be engaged. Linguists have done quite a good job since the mid-1990s under the latter heading: a significant number of people now have a degree of intellectual understanding of the issues which they did not have before. But how many have an emotional grasp? How many would weep over a dying language, as people have wept over a dying animal species. How many experience real joy at the prospect of a revitalized language – like the moment in *Beyond Babel* when we hear Cally Lara, a teenager from Hupa Valley in Northern California, say: 'As long as we're

here, as long as the valley is here, as long as our culture is
alive, the language and teaching the language will be a part
of what we do. It's our responsibility.' And his chum, Silis-
chi-tawn Jackson, adds: 'If it's up to me, this language is
going to go on.' This makes the heart, as well as the mind,
leap, to hear teenagers engage with language issues in this
way. (Anyone who has had teenagers of their own knows
how difficult it is to get them to engage in anything, apart
from sex!) How many share in this sense of celebration?
Indeed, how many opportunities are there to celebrate?
And how many are aware of these opportunities – such as
World Language Day or World International Language
Day? The answer to all these questions must be: still very
few. This is the challenge for the new century.

There is evidently a gap between linguistic consciousness and conscience. We have to engage with people's
sensibilities, and this is the most difficult of tasks. I know
of only two ways of doing it – one is through religion, the
other is through the arts. And of the two, the arts turn out
to be the more general, because they transcend the distinction between theism and a-theism. As director of an arts
centre in my home town, I have learned, from our programme of art exhibitions, sculptures, films, plays, con-
certs and performances of all shapes and sizes, that
everyone appreciates the arts, regardless of age and class.
They may appreciate different kinds of art, of course; but
even the people in my town who turn their noses up at an
exhibition of abstract art or a concert of medieval music,
calling it elitist, come to the arts centre when it is showing
a James Bond film or putting on a Christmas pantomime
for the children. And I have never seen a house without
some sort of picture on the wall or ornament on the
mantelpiece. Art reaches out to everyone. As Oscar
Wilde said, 'We spend our days, each one of us, in looking
for the secret of life. Well, the secret of life is in art.'[1]

So, if we want a means of getting the message about endangered languages across to everyone in the most direct and engaging way, we should be making maximum use of the arts. Artists can help us more than anyone else.[2] Repeatedly we find people acknowledging the point: US poet Archibald Macleish put it like this: 'Anything can make us look; only art can make us see.' Another poet, Robert Penn Warren, wrote: 'the poem is not a thing we see – it is, rather, a light by which we may see – and what we see is life.' Picasso commented: 'We all know that art is not truth. Art is a lie that makes us realize truth.' And, as if drawing attention to the difference between the media and the arts, we have Ezra Pound: 'Literature is news that stays news.' Perhaps the most apposite quotation, in this connection, is from Disraeli, in the Preface to his novel *Coningsby*: 'Fiction, in the temper of the times, stands the best chance of influencing opinion.' I conclude, from this array of opinions, that the best way forward is through the arts, in its broadest sense, to include everything sensory – visual, verbal, tactile, gustatory and olfactory – that we consider artistic. But here we meet the Great Divide in its harshest reality. For academic linguists have not been much interested in the arts, and artists (in this broadest sense) have not been much interested in linguistics.

Since the 1990s I have been trying to find examples of artists who have addressed the issue of language death within their areas of expertise, and I have found next to nothing. I have asked hundreds of artists if they know of anything in the visual arts, and hardly any do. I have seen whole exhibitions devoted to plant and animal conservation, but never seen one which deals with language conservation. I know of some paintings on the general theme of language, such as Hammond Guthrie's *WithOutWords*, published in an issue of the avant-garde on-line magazine

The Third Page (Winter/Spring 2002) on the theme of *Non Angoro Vorto* ('No fear of words'). But nothing on language death. I have come across one sculpture – the living sculpture produced by Rachel Berwick, shown in New York and London, in which two Amazon parrots in a special enclosure had been trained to speak some words of now-extinct Maypuré. I know of nothing in photography or ceramics or textiles. Artists are continually using the terms of language to define their roles – the 'language of' photography, paintings which 'speak to us'. But they do not seem to have focused on language itself as a subject.

I would have expected music and dance to be especially involved in this topic. Music has been characterized[3] as 'the universal language of mankind' (Longfellow), 'the speech of angels' (Carlyle), 'the only universal tongue' (Samuel Rogers). We would expect these metaphors to have motivated composers to reach for their staves to deal with linguistic issues. But I have not yet encountered pieces which deal with the subject explicitly, apart from a short electronic live performance piece by French composer Jean Vauget: 'instant sonore #5 pygmées'. The topic of language death deserves at least a symphony, a fantasia, an opera, a ballet or – to change the genres – a large-scale jazz piece, or a guitar extravaganza. Even the folk-singers have failed to lament about the world situation. The nearest a major musical work comes to the subject is the score Philip Glass composed for Godfrey Reggio's film *Powaqqatsi*, the second of his Hopi *qatsi* trilogy – the name means 'a way of life [technology, in this vision] that consumes the life forces of other beings in order to further its own life'. The anthem composed for that film well expresses the notion of loss, but Reggio's theme is cultural destruction in general, as a result of technology, not linguistic loss in particular. Film itself, as a medium, also seems to have ignored the general topic.

We might expect, from its nature, that the world of the verbal arts would yield more positive results – the world of poetry, drama, the novel, the short story. Here too, though, there is very little. I know of no novel directly concerned with the general theme, though a few which reflect on an individual cultural or linguistic situation – such as Joan Bodon (Jean Boudou) writing on the death of Occitan (e.g. *Lo Libre de Catoia*), the Argentinian writer Leopoldo Brizuela's fable about an imaginary encounter between English and Patagonian cultures (*Inglaterra, una fabula*), or the Abkhazian writer Bagrat Shinkuba's account of the demise of Ubykh (translated as *Last of the Departed*). There is Alphonse Daudet's short story 'The Last Class', about the reaction of a schoolchild to the news that French was being replaced by German in his Alsatian school. But there seems to be no novel on the general theme – and only one short story, by the Australian writer David Malouf. In a succinct, breathtaking four-page tale, 'The Only Speaker of his Tongue', he tells the story of a lexicographer visiting a last speaker. When the scholar eventually meets the man, their encounter prompts a moment of personal reflection: 'When I think of my tongue being no longer alive in the mouths of men, a chill goes over me that is deeper than my own death, since it is the gathered death of all my kind.'[4] This is poetry in prose. And, to move into the genre of poetry, here a few writers *have* taken the theme on board. I have been collecting poems on the subject, and so far have about thirty. From Canada we have Margaret Atwood, whose 'Marsh Language' stands out. It begins:

> The dark soft languages are being silenced:
> Mothertongue Mothertongue Mothertongue
> falling one by one back into the moon.[5]

The US author W.C. Merwin has written a handful
of relevant poems. Here is the beginning of 'Losing a
Language':

> A breath leaves the sentences and does not come back
> yet the old still remember something that they could say[6]

What is important about such poems is that they are
generalizing works. They are not restricted to bemoaning
the plight of the author's own language, and stopping with
that. They use a personal experience to reflect upon the
world situation. Some authors are very skilled at doing
this. One of the poets in Wales who repeatedly wrote in
this way was R.S. Thomas, an Anglican clergyman. He
was desperately concerned about the loss of Welsh,
but note how, in this poem, 'Drowning', his reflections
at the very end leave Wales, and become of general
applicability:

> They were irreplaceable and forgettable.
> Inhabitants of the parish and speakers
> of the Welsh tongue, I looked on and
> there was one less and one less and one less.
>
> They were not of the soil, but contributed
> to it in dying, a manure not
> to be referred to as such, but from which
> poetry is grown and legends and green tales.
>
> Their immortality was what they hoped for
> by being kind. Their smiles were such as,
> exercised so often, became perennial
> as flowers, blossoming where they had been cut down.
>
> I ministered uneasily among them until
> what had been gaps in the straggling hedgerow

of the nation widened to reveal the emptiness
that was inside, where echoes haunted and thin ghosts.

A rare place, but one identifiable
with other places where on as deep a sea
men have clung to the last spars of their language
and gone down with it, unremembered but uncomplaining.[7]

The point could not be clearer: this is a people and a language 'identifiable with other places', and the image of the drowning language would resonate anywhere.

But the genre which puzzles me most, because it is the genre most obviously applicable to expound the subject of language death, is theatre. Where are the plays? Here too there have been works which deal with the problems of a particular linguistic/cultural situation – a well-known example is Brian Friel's *Translations*, about Irish. Another is Louis Nowra's *The Golden Age*, about the community discovered in the wilds of Tasmania in 1939, for whom the playwright created a special variety of speech. But which plays deal with the problems of language endangerment in general, or which generalize from individual instances in the way R.S. Thomas's poem did? Harold Pinter's *Mountain Language*, a twenty-minute virtuoso explosion, is the only published instance, but that is of little general use for it deals only with the topic of linguistic genocide, which, relevant as it is for some parts of the world, is only a part of the overall picture.

It was because of the lack of professional playwriting contributions to the theme that I followed up a proposal from a British theatre director, Greg Doran, to make a personal contribution to the genre, which resulted in the play *Living On* (1998). This play takes the theme which I consider to be of maximum dramatic potential, that of the 'last speaker'. I created an archetypal character (Shalema)

and community derived from the personalities and traditions which have been studied in many parts of the world,
invented a language, based on linguistic universals, for him
to speak, then explored the motivations and tensions
which affected him as he decides whether to allow his
language to be recorded for posterity or not. The following
extract illustrates Shalema's state of mind as he talks to the
linguist who wants to record his language:

> When I wake up in the morning, my head is no longer full
> of the sound of the rhythms of my language, as once it was.
> Your language is there now, making me think in strange
> ways, forcing my thoughts into strange rhythms. I have
> begun to forget how it was. Every day, I feel my language
> slipping away. The words which were my life are slowly
> leaving me. They are returning to their home, where they
> were born. I could no longer tell our stories well.[8]

Although the play received readings of various kinds, its
subject-matter never attracted the interest of mainstream
theatre.

Perhaps this is not surprising. It appears that language
death is not just 'not mainstream theatre' – it is not mainstream anything. It is so far outside the mindsets of most
people that they have difficulty appreciating what the crisis
is all about, because they are not used to thinking about
language as an issue in itself. Somehow these mindsets
need to be changed. We need to get people thinking
about language more explicitly, more intimately, more
enthusiastically. Interest in language is certainly there, in
the general population – most people are fascinated by
such topics as where words come from, or what the origin
of their town's name is, or whether their baby's name
means anything; they are certainly prepared to play
Scrabble and a host of other language games ad infinitum;

and language games are a major interest on radio and television – but a willingness to focus that interest on general issues, a preparedness to take on board the emotion and drama inherent in the situation of language endangerment, is not something that happens much. This a goal which artists can make attainable.

I believe the arts are the greatest untapped resource that we can exploit to engage public interest in language death. And one of my fondest hopes for the new century is that national and international organizations will introduce language and arts initiatives in which the artists of the world become mobilized to address the theme, using all the resources at their disposal. Artists are extraordinary people. Once you catch their interest you do not have to persuade them to act. By their nature, they cannot not. The trick is to draw their attention to the fact that language, as such, is an issue. This is demonstrated by the work of Lucy Crystal in Amsterdam, in relation to a project called 'Language as Arts and Arts as Language'. She made contact with artists in several European countries, none of whom had ever thought of producing work in relation to this theme, but all of whom proved keen to do so. An array of fine ideas came out of the preliminary thinking, but in the absence of funding the project remained in abeyance. Two achievements have so far arisen from the initiative. In 2002, during a month-long project in Arizona, a small team worked with the rurally isolated youth of three US Amerindian communities – the Hopi, Navajo and Gila – to teach them how to use digital story-telling techniques to record on film aspects of their communities' oral histories.[9] And in 2003, another team made a film of a Neapolitan story-telling ritual (the *Tammurriata*) still practised in towns and villages in parts of southern Italy, focusing on an annual celebration at Maiori, near Naples. Part of a projected series of films called 'Stories from the Edge: the Art of Survival', this initiative demonstrates that there is a great deal of interest, expertise and potential within the artistic community, and I have no doubt that this exists worldwide – but it needs to be tapped.

Give artists an opportunity and they will take it. The problem is that, in so much work, opportunities are missed – not because of any active antagonism towards the language question, but simply because people have just not thought of it as an issue. In 2001 I returned from Brazil with a beautiful glossy art-book of photographs on the country, in which the writer and photographer had gone out of their way to find communities and environments at risk. However, there was not a single mention of the Brazilian language crisis in the whole book. There were statistics about the amount of rainforest which was disappearing, but none about the number of languages which were disappearing. The writer, I suspect, had simply not noticed it, or had taken it for granted, or had forgotten about it. The photographer had not even conceived of the exciting artistic challenge of attempting to pictorialize it.

We need the arts to help us get our initiative into the three domains where it can make greatest impact – the media, the school and the home – and these suggest the kinds of action which need to be taken if we are to make significant progress in reversing the phenomenon of language death. For the media we need a stock of memorable, quotable statements from writers, pop-singers, film-stars and others in the public eye. Linguists are writers themselves, so they can do their bit; but good slogans come best out of the mouths of artists. The media love artists. If a famous artist cuts a little finger it can be headline news with a photograph. If an academic linguist breaks a neck, it might make a late edition, on page 17, at the bottom, misspelled.

For the school, we need to get the issue into the curricula – something which is beginning to happen in a small way. In the UK, for example, the topic of language death is recognized in the A-level English Language syllabus that children begin at age 16. But age 16 is far too late; awareness of the biological crisis is in schools at age 5. Art projects can help here too. There have been entire art exhibitions by children on the theme of wildlife extinction. There need to be language extinction exhibitions too.

But above all we have to get awareness of the language crisis into the home, and there are only two real ways of doing this on a large scale: through the Internet and through the arts. The Internet is an important and still under-used resource for this theme, but, as we saw in chapter 3, it has its problems: it is still not available to a huge proportion of the human race; it can be slow and cumbersome, especially in downloading multimedia material; and those who do use the Internet routinely know how difficult it is to get a simple message across – or even noticed, within the floods of pages that exist. But the arts can get into the home every day in all kinds of mutually reinforcing ways – whether it be via a radio or television programme, a CD or DVD, a computer game, a wall decoration or painting or photograph, a novel, a post-card or a text-message poem (currently one of the coolest of artistic mediums among the young). There are so many opportunities, and so few have yet been exploited.

An example is Christmas – but the same principle can apply to non-Christian festivals – when many homes receive Christmas cards. Several are bilingual or multilingual, but the languages are all healthy languages, full of *joyeux Noël*s and *fröhliche Weihnachten*s. There seem to be no Xmas cards in which last speakers wish us happy holidays in their languages – possibly for the last time? There seem to be no cards wishing us happiness in Aramaic, the language of Jesus and his disciples, a language which is so near to extinction in the present-day Middle East that, if he were to return using his mother-tongue, he would soon find no-one able to understand him.

None of the major issues raised by language endangerment and death seem to have received artistic treatment. Has there ever been an artistic oeuvre in which we see portrayed, for example, the communication gap between grandparent and grandchild, or any of the other striking images which we know characterize this field? There is certainly no shortage of images. In a poem, 'It Hurts Him to Think', R.S. Thomas writes:

> The
> industrialists came, burrowing
> in the corpse of a nation
> for its congealed blood. I was
> born into the squalor of
> their feeding and sucked their speech
> in with my mother's
> infected milk, so that whatever
> I throw up now is still theirs.[10]

An image such as 'my mother's linguistically infected milk' cries out for imaginative portrayal in other media. Or again, in 'Reservoirs' he writes:

> I have walked the shore
> For an hour and seen the English
> Scavenging among the remains
> Of our culture, covering the sand
> Like the tide and, with the roughness
> Of the tide, elbowing our language
> Into the grave that we have dug for it.[11]

'Elbowing a language into a grave' is another striking image. And there are many such dramatic and memorable images in the slowly growing poetic literature. In some cases people might find these images shocking. They might even offend their sensibilities. But at least they would have made people sit up and take notice.

Alongside the properly technical concerns of language documentation and analysis, therefore, initiatives for the new century need to focus on communication with the general public. Collaboration between linguistics and the world of the arts and media is the most promising way forward, and means need to be found of making this collaboration easier. At the very least, there needs to be an archive or library of data about endangered languages, accessible to journalists, broadcasters and artists, so that they can easily find examples of what is happening in order to make their point. One means of doing this would be to establish a public depository, such as exists in the book world, for copies of works – radio programmes, magazine articles, interviews with last speakers and community leaders, stock footage of communities – anything which relates to language death. Then positive steps need to be taken to attract the interest of artists. One way would be a prize. Modern society is obsessed with prizes – Oscars, Grammies, Emmies, Golden Globes, Bookers, Pulitzers, Goncourts . . . The annual award of the Turner prize, in its often controversial decisions, has generated an extraordinary amount of discussion about the nature of art. There needs to be a prize for artistic achievement in endangered languages. It could be announced on World Language Day.

5

Language Themes for the Twenty-First Century

Because there was so much linguistic innovation and change in the 1990s, several of our assumptions about language which we took for granted in the twentieth century are having to be revised for the twenty-first. The arrival of a global language, English, has altered the balance of linguistic power in unprecedented ways, and generated a whole new set of attitudes about language and languages. Many speech communities have begun to feel threatened by a situation which can alter the character of their language, or, in the worst case, cause the use of their language to become so reduced that its very survival is at risk. Several are finding it necessary to introduce protective policies, or at least to find ways of managing the effects of the linguistic changes they are experiencing. At an international level, such as in the European Union, more sophisticated strategies are having to be implemented to safeguard the principle of language equivalence while recognizing the practical fact that virtually everyone speaks English. At the same time, communities want to exploit the opportunities for empowerment opened up by the availability of an international lingua franca. They find themselves having to take fresh measures, such as devoting resources to English language teaching, introducing an English-language dimension at senior levels of management (at least, for corporations which have an international remit), and ensuring that their tourist potential is maintained by incorporating an English interpreting facility into important venues.

Then, within the community of English users itself there is also a degree of turmoil, as speakers (including learners and their teachers) find they have to get to grips with a rapidly diversifying language, in which evolving regional standards and an increasing number of 'New Englishes' complicate a world where once only British and American English ruled. The process of change, moreover, has been radically affected by the arrival of the Internet, which has not only given humanity a third medium of communication, whose potentialities have hardly begun to be exploited, but has also initiated a process of graphic translation, from paper to screen, of all previous styles of written language, and motivated the emergence of brand-new linguistic varieties, in the form of Netspeak. Here too there is a need for fresh policies and strategies. Teachers of English as a foreign language are finding they must broaden the remit of their activities to give their students exposure to new varieties and forms of English, a process which will become more focused as teaching materials and examination systems adopt a global perspective. And mother-tongue teachers too are having to adapt, as they find themselves needing to replace a previously exclusive attention to the standard language with an approach which pays respectful attention to regional accents and dialects, both nationally and internationally. But it is not only teaching which is affected. Everyone has to come to terms with the linguistic potential (for good and evil) of the Internet, and to devise appropriate management strategies – such as in relation to the legal status of its documents, or the copyright position of creative work.

The prominence of English on the world stage, and the role of the Internet in contemporary society, in their different ways both reflect the same process of globalization which has caused such havoc in relation to the planet's linguistic diversity. There is no doubt that the crisis facing the world's languages is unprecedented in its scale and urgency, and in the twenty-first century is the main responsibility facing those governments, international organizations, philanthropists, artists and activists who profess to acknowledge the importance of language in their lives. The fact that a language is becoming extinct, somewhere in the world, around every two weeks dwarfs the scale of species endangerment in botany and zoology, and cries out for special action. The situation is being helped by the way the Internet has evolved in such a short time to provide a tool for the use of many minority and endangered languages – offering a level of expressive capability that their communities could never have dreamed of a decade ago. But the technology is simply not available to help two-thirds or more of the languages that are most in danger, so alternative strategies have to be found. We know from the activities that have gone on around the world in the past few years that documentation and revitalization can be successfully carried out if the political and financial will are present. That is the chief linguistic challenge of the new century. The 2003 UNESCO conference on language endangerment was an important step in the right direction, but whether it proves to be a small step or a large one remains to be seen.

The three trends of my revolutionary decade interrelate in all kinds of ways, and indicate the importance of a further perspective. Taking action to promote, support, protect, manage, teach and fund languages presupposes a certain awareness of the nature of language as such. What is language? How did speech evolve in the human race?

How does it develop in the individual human being? How did reading and writing develop? How is language structured? In how many ways can language be used? Are there properties of sound, or grammar, or meaning found in all languages? Such questions are the be-all and end-all of linguistics, but they go well beyond linguistics in their general interest and relevance to the solution of everyday language problems. For everyone, at some point or other, has to deal with the issues and procedures introduced by mother-tongue or foreign-language learning, translating and interpreting, using dictionaries, ensuring precision and clarity of expression, and a host of other practical tasks in which the ability to produce and understand language is critical to success or failure. It may seem like a truism, but it still needs to be said: everyone, in an age of global communication, needs to be language-aware.

Schools can and do help, especially since the 1990s, when in several parts of the world new curricula began to draw children's attention to the principles and practices of language study in fresh and interesting ways. But there is still a noticeable absence of institutions capable of meeting the mature curiosity and needs of an adult population. It is interesting to compare the way in which other curricular domains are treated. If we are interested in botany, zoology, geology, textiles, transport, history, the arts, science or technology, we can feed our interest by visiting an appropriate museum, exhibition hall, gallery, arena or other space devoted to the subject. Every major city has an art gallery of some kind, or a natural history museum. But where is the 'gallery' devoted to language? Where is the space where people could go to see how language works, how it is used, and how languages evolve?

The 1990s in the UK was revolutionary in one further respect. A group of experts came up with the idea for a 'World of Language', which would fill this gap. It would have been a multi-storey building, the first of its kind, with floors devoted to the world of speech, the world of writing, the world of meaning, the world of languages and the world of language study. A building had even been identified, in Southwark, right next to Shakespeare's Globe. The plans had reached an advanced stage, with the support of the British Council, and all that was required was a small tranche of government funding to get the project off the ground. Things were looking promising. But then the government had a better idea. It was called the Millennium Dome.

The money which was wasted on the Dome project would have supported twenty 'worlds of language'. We still have none. Abroad, others have come up with similar ideas. The various projects have a variety of names, such as 'the language city', and 'the town as a linguistic landscape'. A few already exist, but on a very small scale, such as the Kiev Language Educational Museum. In several countries, the subject of language forms a part of a broader remit, such as at the Heureka Museum in Finland and the Japanese National Museum of Ethnology in Osaka. Many museums, of course, including some in the UK, have sections devoted to the history of writing. And there are also several virtual projects, such as the Virtual Museum of American Linguistic Heritage, and 'The House of Languages', an initiative of the European Centre for Modern Languages. But all projects suffer from a lack of finance, and few have got past the proposal stage. Despite the avowedly fundamental role of language in relation to human society and thought, there is an extraordinary reluctance to give it the public educational treatment it demands.

We still await the arrival of the world's first comprehensive 'Language Gallery', and perhaps the twenty-first century will produce it. In the meantime, I conclude by reflecting on the main preoccupations which should be characterizing the linguistic mindset of the new millennium:

I   The top priority has to be a greater concern for endangered languages. The concern can take many forms – aside from doing the actual work of linguistic documentation – such as lobbying for political support, providing help at community level and fundraising. All speakers, and especially those whose languages are *not* in any danger (at present), should be reflecting on this, and doing something about it.

II   Close behind comes a greater concern for minority languages, even if they are not in any global sense endangered. All languages express the identity of the people who speak them, but for those who find themselves to be a small part of a large community, the role of language is especially important. They want to see their language treated with respect by the dominant culture; they want opportunities (which usually means funding) to use their language in public and see it valued. It would be intellectually dishonest to take pride in the achievements of one's own language while denying the same opportunity to others.

III We need to promote a greater concern for all accents and dialects within a language. Here we are talking about a readiness to accept the variety of forms a language takes as it varies from one part of a country to another. We do not have to personally like all these forms, any more than we have to like all kinds of music or literature. But we should not go round, as many have done, condemning some (usually urban) dialects as ugly, rough or slovenly, or their speakers as unintelligent or criminal. 'Eternal vigilance' was once the slogan of a puristic and prescriptively minded linguistic age, which was steadily losing its appeal in the closing years of the twentieth century. The linguistic slogan of the new century should be 'eternal tolerance'.

IV At the same time, we need to promote a greater concern for the expressive range of a language. This means valuing all varieties and styles in a language, whether spoken or written, formal or informal, regional or social, domestic or professional. It means being concerned over standards of excellence, while recognizing that language reflects many needs and activities. One of the purposes of language is to express identity, as we have seen; another is to foster mutual intelligibility. This means that language has to be clear, care has to be taken to avoid ambiguity, and subtleties of expression have to be carefully managed. There has long been a concern in schools for children to master a standard language, in which the focus is on the sounds, grammar and vocabulary that facilitate national (and, these days, international) intelligibility. In the past, this was all too often seen as a replacement for a local dialect. The new mindset sees the value of both.[1]

V   We need to become more multilingual in our thinking, and in our abilities. There are still too many cultures which are monolingual in temperament. These – though they may not realize it – are the disadvantaged ones. Although culturally dominant, reflecting their colonial pasts, they are missing out intellectually by failing to make a second language a routine part of growing up. Let us recall, from chapter 2, the words of Emerson: 'As many languages as he has, as many friends, as many arts and trades, so many times is he a man.' Or woman. And the benefits, as people are beginning to learn, can be economic as well as personal.

VI   We need to accept change in language as a normal process. This means we should stop seeing it as decay and deterioration, and complaining about it to the press, the prime minister or whoever we hope will listen. There is probably more time wasted on this issue than on any other in the world of language. Language change is inevitable, continuous, universal and multidirectional. Languages do not get better or worse when they change. They just change.

VII   We need to show greater concern for those who are having difficulties learning their mother-tongue – whether for medical, psychological or other reasons. As many as ten per cent of the child population can be affected by handicaps in listening, speaking, reading or writing. Deafness, cleft palate, dyslexia and language delay are just some of the conditions which form the world of another cadre of language professionals, the speech and language pathologists. That is a world where there is a shortage of funding too.

VIII   We need to show greater concern for those who have lost their ability to use a mother-tongue in which they were once proficient. This is the language pathology world also, but now we are talking about the linguistic consequences of strokes, and other forms of brain damage, among the adult population. Aphasia is one of the best-known syndromes, but there are several other difficulties, such as stammering, which need both sympathetic understanding and serious research.

IX   We need to bring the study of language and literature closer together. All too often, schools, universities and language-teaching institutions introduce a sharp boundary between the two domains. 'The language' is taught in one class; 'the literature' in another. It is time to allow more language awareness into the literature class, and more literary awareness into the language class. Both sides, after all, have a focus on creativity. Language develops and changes through the creation of new words and sentences; literature, through the creation of new discourses.

X   Finally, we need to appreciate, truly appreciate, the value of language in human development and society. Languages should be thought of as national treasures, and treated accordingly.

Notes

Chapter 1   The Future of Englishes

1   Letter to the President of Congress (5 September 1780), in C.F. Adams (ed.), *The Works of John Adams* (Boston: Little, Brown, 1852), p. 250.

2   Three books focused the debate: my own *English as a Global Language* (Cambridge: Cambridge University Press, 1997, 2nd edn 2003), on which this chapter is based; David Graddol, *The Future of English* (London: The British Council, 1998); and Tom McArthur, *The English Languages* (Cambridge: Cambridge University Press, 1998).

3   Reported in Geoffrey Nunberg, 'Will the Internet always speak English?' *American Prospect* 11(10), 27 March–10 April 2000.

4   Reported in David Robinson, 'The Hollywood conquest', *Encyclopedia Britannica Book of the Year* (1995), p. 245.

5   Sridath Ramphal, 'World language: opportunities, challenges, responsibilities', paper given at the World Members' Conference of the English-Speaking Union, Harrogate, UK, 1996.

6   Jean and William Branford (eds), *A Dictionary of South African English* (Cape Town: Oxford University Press, 1978); Joan Hughes (ed.), *The Concise Australian National Dictionary* (Melbourne: Oxford University Press, 1989); F.G. Cassidy

and R.B. Le Page (eds), *Dictionary of Jamaican English* (Cambridge: Cambridge University Press, 1967).

7 Tom McArthur, *The English Languages* (Cambridge: Cambridge University Press), p. 13.

8 Richard Mulcaster, *The First Part of the Elementarie* (1582, edited by E.T. Campagnac, Oxford, 1925), p. 256.

Chapter 2 The Future of Languages

1 Manfred Görlach, *A Dictionary of European Anglicisms* (Oxford: Oxford University Press, 2000), pp. 1–2.

2 See David Crystal, *Language Death* (Cambridge: Cambridge University Press, 2000), on which this chapter – apart from the first section – is based.

3 See Dónall Ó Riagáin (ed.), *Vade-Mecum: A Guide to Legal, Political and Other Official International Documents Pertaining to the Lesser Used Languages of Europe* (Dublin: European Bureau for Lesser Used Languages).

4 Oliver Wendell Holmes, Sr, *The Professor at the Breakfast Table* (Boston: Ticknor and Fields, 1860), p. 46.

5 In James Boswell, *The Journal of a Tour to the Hebrides* (London: Charles Dilly, 1785), recorded on 18 September 1773.

6 Ezra Pound, *The ABC of Reading* (New York: Laughlin, 1960 [1934]), p. 1.

7 George Steiner, *Language and Silence* (London: Faber and Faber, 1967), p. 264.

8 Ralph Waldo Emerson, *The Conduct of Life* (London: Dent, Everyman's Library edn, 1963 [1860]), essay on 'Culture', p. 221.

9 Recommendations to UNESCO for Action Plans for the Safeguarding of Endangered Languages (Paris-Fontenoy: UNESCO, March 2003).

Chapter 3   The Role of the Internet

1 In *Language and the Internet* (Cambridge: Cambridge University Press, 2001), on which this chapter is based.
2 Respectively: Philip Elmer-Dewitt, 'Bards of the Internet', *Time*, 4 July 1994, pp. 66–7; Constance Hale and Jessie Scanlon, *Wired Style: Principles of English Usage in the Digital Age* (New York: Broadway Books, 1999), p. 3; John Naughton, *A Brief History of the Future: The Origins of the Internet* (London: Weidenfeld and Nicolson, 1999), p. 143.
3 *The Simpsons*, episode 12A6.
4 Tim Berners-Lee, *Weaving the Web* (London: Orion Business Books, 1999), p. 132.
5 John Naughton, *A Brief History of the Future: The Origins of the Internet* (London: Weidenfeld and Nicolson, 1999), p. 150.
6 Berners-Lee, *Weaving the Web*, p. 151.
7 Michael Specter, 'World, Wide, Web: 3 English words', *The New York Times*, 14 April 1996, pp. 4–5.
8 Ned Thomas, 'How much IT can minority languages afford?' *Contact*, 16(3), 2000, p. 2.
9 Cited in Marie-France Lebert, *Le multilinguisme sur le Web* (1999) <*http://www.ceveil.qc.ca/ multi0.htm*>.

Chapter 4   After the Revolution

1 In *Nothing – Except My Genius* (Harmondsworth: Penguin, 1997), p. 4.
2 The following quotations are, respectively, from Macleish: 'Riverside', in *Poetry and Experience* (New York: Houghton Mifflin, 1961), p. 10; Warren: *Saturday Review* (22 March 1958); Picasso: in Dore Ashton, *Picasso on Art* (Cambridge, MA: Da Capo Press, 1972), p. 25; Pound: *The ABC of Reading* (New York: Laughlin, 1960 [1934]), p. 29.

3   From, respectively, Longfellow: *Outre-Mer* (1833–5); Car-
     lyle: *The Opera* (1852); Rogers: *Italy* (1822–8), in Derek
     Watson (ed.), *Chambers Music Quotations* (Edinburgh:
     Chambers, 1991), pp. 7, 4, 8, respectively.
4   In *Antipodes* (London: Chatto & Windus, 1985), p. 70.
5   In *Morning in the Burned House* (Houghton Mifflin, 1995),
     p. 19.
6   In *The Rain in the Trees* (New York: Knopf, 1999), p. 67.
7   In *Collected Poems 1945–90* (London: Phoenix Press, 2001),
     p. 464.
8   *Living On* (1998: available from the author).
9   See the diary account at *<http://www.rez02.net>*.
10   In *Collected Poems 1945–90*, p. 262.
11   Ibid., p. 194.

Chapter 5   Language Themes for the Twenty-First Century

1   This mindset is the theme of my *The Stories of English*
     (London: Penguin, 2004).

Index